OUTDOOR KITCHENS

QUARRY

OUTDOOR KITCHENS

Designs for Outdoor Kitchens, Bars, and Dining Areas

GLOUCESTER MASSACHUSETTS

QUARRY BOOKS

Amanda Lecky

First published in the United States of America by
Quarry Books, a member of
Quayside Publishing Group
33 Commercial Street
Gloucester, Massachusetts 01930-5089
Telephone: (978) 282-9590
Fax: (978) 283-2742
www.rockpub.com

Library of Congress Cataloging-in-Publication Data
Lecky, Amanda.
   Outdoor kitchens : designs for outdoor kitchens, bars, and dining areas / Amanda Lecky.
      p.   cm.
   ISBN 1-59253-203-9 (pbk.)
   1. Outdoor living spaces. 2. Kitchens. 3. Dining rooms. I. Title.
   NK2117.O87L43 2005
   747'.8893-dc22   2005010368
                                                                          CIP

ISBN 1-59253-203-9

10 9 8 7 6 5 4 3 2 1

Book Design: *tabula rasa* graphic design
Cover Image: Fred Stocker/Jean McCabe, Stylist
Back cover: Illustration by Robert Leanna II; Courtesy of Rod Mickley Interior Design, (middle); Courtesy of KitchenAid, (right)

Printed in China

For Tom, my favorite outdoor cook, and his talented assistants, John and Wyatt

CONTENTS

INTRODUCTION

One Christmas morning my three-year-old son discovered that Santa had left him a king's ransom of gifts. His favorite? Not the castle (though he does love to yell "Raise the portcullis!") nor the books nor the football. Nope, it was the plastic kettle grill, complete with glowing "coals" that make a sizzling sound as you move the pretend food across the grate. We're still eating perfectly prepared rubber hot dogs ... nine months later.

Apparently, there's something about cooking with fire that appeals to most people, regardless of their age. And it's been that way since time immemorial. No one really knows how humans discovered the pleasures of eating flame-broiled meat—some postulate that our prehistoric forebears stumbled across the concept when they found animals killed in a forest fire—but we can all agree on its allure. After all, nearly every nation on earth enjoys its own form (or forms) of live-fire cooking, from the quick satays grilled by the street vendors of Thailand to the rich steaks seared to perfection by Argentine grillmasters. American homeowners have long manned their backyard barbecues just as diligently; over the years outdoor cooking and living has gained such popularity that it has spawned a whole new "room": the outdoor kitchen.

Much as the indoor kitchen has, in recent years, assumed the role of the heart of the home, functioning as far more than a place to prepare meals, the outdoor kitchen can—and should—be the anchor of an outdoor living space, where family and friends can relax in comfort while enjoying the great outdoors. But, as you might expect, designing an outdoor kitchen can be complicated. Not only must you apply the same principles you would to an indoor kitchen—

careful layout, smart appliance and materials choices—but the space will have to contend with challenges from the weather, and its design must flow well with existing elements such as patios, decks, and pools, as well as mesh with the style of your house. Don't fret: *Outdoor Kitchens* gives you all the information you need to design a space that meets and exceeds your expectations on every front—cooking, living, and entertaining, all in style—starting with the basics: planning and design.

In chapter one, you'll learn how to decide which features are must-haves and which you can live without; how to finance your project; and how to determine the best location and layout for the space. Chapter two moves on to the fun stuff: shopping for the appliances and materials that will make your outdoor kitchen hum with efficiency. Chapter three focuses on your friends and family, and helps you plan the perfect place to entertain—on a small or large scale. Style comes into play in chapter four, where we'll discuss finding the look that's right for you and take a peek at several popular styles. Chapter five covers practical matters such as lighting and climate control (and even preempting pests). Chapter six gets at the heart of the matter—the products that will give your space its style and substance—and chapter seven helps you do it yourself, with instructions for three outdoor kitchen projects: tiling a countertop, building an arbor, and constructing a grill island. Throughout, you'll find interviews with celebrity chefs who love their own outdoor kitchens; tips from experienced kitchen designers; and beautiful, inspirational photographs.

Enjoy—and bon appètit!

CHAPTER ONE

TAKE IT OUTSIDE
DESIGNING THE PERFECT OUTDOOR KITCHEN

Close your eyes and imagine this: The weather is warm, the sky is clear, and you're cooking in your new outdoor kitchen. Everything you need is at hand; the look is just right; you couldn't be more pleased with the layout, design, and appliances. Note what you're cooking, and for whom. Pay attention to the way you feel, how you're dressed, and the time of day. Hold this perfect tableau in your mind for a few moments—then open your eyes. Congratulations—the easy part of designing your own outdoor kitchen is over.

FINDING YOUR OUTDOOR COOKING STYLE

Deciding that you want an outdoor kitchen is simple; actually creating an efficient, attractive cooking and entertaining space that you'll use and enjoy requires a bit more effort. So, go back to that image of your ideal outdoor kitchen and evaluate it, one step at a time. First, how much—or how little—do you really need? You may have imagined yourself whipping up a feast in a fully outfitted, built-in outdoor kitchen like celebrity chef Bobby Flay's rooftop kitchen featured on his TV grilling show, but if you use your grill only for Sunday cookouts two months out of the year, your home-improvement funds are probably best allocated else-where. You'll be happy with a fairly basic setup that includes a freestanding grill and maybe a portable prep table. If, on the other hand, you spend several months a year eating and entertaining outdoors, and you'd like to cook full meals—including side dishes—outdoors, you'll probably feel that investing in a deluxe outdoor cooking space with, for instance, a built-in grill, refrigerator, cabinetry, and a prep sink is a worthwhile addition to your home.

Your lifestyle is as important a consideration as your outdoor cooking style, so think about the different ways you will use the new space, and plan accordingly. For example, if you love the bold flavors of grilled food but prefer to eat and entertain indoors, you can focus on creating a simple, but well-equipped, grilling area and forgo outdoor dining and lounging

A well-designed outdoor kitchen should be efficient and attractive, and, above all, versatile. Easy access to the indoor kitchen is a must, and a dining area adds comfort and functionality.

How you plan to use your outdoor kitchen will help determine its location. Here, the grilling area is compact, but well equipped, and accessible from the porch—yet tucked away from the flow of traffic.

spaces. Many homeowners, however, find themselves using outdoor spaces such as patios and decks, as outdoor living rooms throughout much of the year.

If this sounds like your family, it makes sense to design an outdoor kitchen that's as welcoming and inviting as your indoor kitchen, with a mix of food-prep and hangout zones. You might, for example, plan a galley-style workspace with the appliances along the wall of the house, opposite a long two-level island with storage beneath the counter, a prep sink at the work level, and a snack or cocktail bar along the second level. Stools that pull up to the bar let family and friends stay close to the cook without getting underfoot. An adjacent dining table and maybe an all-weather sofa and some comfy chairs would round out this full-scale outdoor great room.

The scale of the cooking, dining, and lounging areas depends on how many people will use the space. Family get-togethers may require seating only for eight or ten; hosting large, catered events will mean providing space for buffets,

multiple tables, and even tents. Setup and cleanup are important considerations as well. Do you want to carry dishes and flatware out from the indoor kitchen, or does it make more sense to store them at the point of use? If the latter has more appeal, you'll need to incorporate cabinetry into your plan. Keep in mind that cold temperatures can crack delicate porcelain, so this is only a warm-weather option; or, plan to bring breakables inside for the winter. And what about washing up after a meal? Unless you want to move everything back inside after dinner, you'll want to plan a cleanup zone.

Think also about the kinds of activities that go on around the outdoor kitchen. For instance, if your outdoor kitchen will be near a pool area, it can be a good idea to combine it with a pool house—an especially wise plan if you live in a cold climate where you'll need to protect the grill and other appliances for a portion of each year—but you might want to enclose the cooking and eating area with a fence to keep small children from straying too close to the water's edge during cookouts.

BURNING QUESTIONS

Understanding how you'll use the new space will help you decide how to outfit it, so start by asking yourself the following questions:

1. How many months of each year—realistically—will I cook outdoors?

2. How much space can I allocate to an outdoor kitchen? Should it stand alone or be connected to the house?

3. Is there easy access to the indoor kitchen?

4. Can I incorporate shelter from the elements?

5. Do I want to winterize the space, or should some elements be portable? Alternatively, should I leave the appliances outside but disconnect them from power, gas, and water lines in winter?

6. What will I cook outdoors? Simple things such as hamburgers or full meals, including side dishes?

7. Are there specialty items—such as bread, pizza, or seafood—I'd like to prepare outdoors?

8. Will I also eat outdoors? How often?

9. Will I entertain in the space? How large a group?

10. What look do I want—traditional? rustic? contemporary?

A freestanding outdoor kitchen is a great choice for homeowners who entertain frequently, because it allows guests to circulate freely around an open area. Be sure to plan hangout zones, such as a bar and dining area, as well.

Even the simplest outdoor kitchen should have ample counterspace. Plan at least two dedicated areas: one for preparing foods and another "landing" space for setting hot dishes.

By now you should have a fairly good idea of what combination of cooking, dining, lounging, and bar spaces you want your project to include. We'll talk about the entertainment areas in detail later; let's start with the most important part: the prep zone. Like any indoor kitchen, a successful outdoor cooking space is one that's custom-matched to its chef: you. Take the time to do a little soul searching. First, exactly what will you be cooking in this outdoor kitchen? Burgers and hot dogs on a sunny Sunday afternoon? Slow-cooked barbecue? An entire pig? A smoked

turkey? Bread? Pizza? Maybe you'd like to preserve your garden's bounty without overheating your indoor kitchen. Perhaps you'd like to be able to stir-fry vegetables to serve alongside grilled chicken satay for an easy Asian menu. Or maybe you plan to heat a delicate sauce—or simmer a low-country boil—on an auxiliary burner. The appliances you choose for your kitchen depend entirely on the foods you plan to cook there, so think carefully.

Next, consider how you like to cook outdoors. Do you want to cook everything outside, or finish the side dishes in

STEVEN RAICHLEN

Award-winning author, journalist, cooking teacher, and TV host Steven Raichlen has written twenty-five cookbooks, including the best-selling *The Barbecue Bible,* an IACP/Julia Child Award-winning study of global grilling, and *How To Grill,* a step-by-step guide to live-fire cooking. He began his career with a Thomas J. Watson Foundation Fellowship to study medieval cooking in Europe (along with a Fulbright scholarship to study comparative literature). More recently, Raichlen has turned his scholarship to grilling, presiding over Barbecue University at the Greenbrier resort in White Sulfur Springs, West Virginia, for which *Bon Appètit* magazine named him Cooking Teacher of the Year in 2003. As host of the PBS cooking show *Barbecue University with Steven Raichlen,* Raichlen puts his students through the paces of a rigorous introduction to the art and craft of live-fire cooking.

Professional Help

Steven Raichlen has a deep connection to the bold flavors of food cooked outdoors, and his outdoor kitchen is a grilling enthusiast's dream—though it might lose points for style.

"My wife complains that my outdoor kitchen looks like a hardware store," he says. "It's a collection of the best of each kind of grill—like a gallery of constantly changing exhibits. We're all about function, not form, here." Raichlen's "hardware store" might at any given time include some combination of gas and charcoal grills, including an infrared grill; a large barrel smoker for true barbecue; and a ceramic Kamado-style cooker—an ancient Asian grill updated for modern performance (see page 48).

He has plenty of good advice for an amateur chef setting up an outdoor kitchen at home. "First, decide how much grilling you're going to be doing. Get a big gas grill for every night and at least one charcoal cooking device, because it's virtually impossible to smoke on a gas grill. If you entertain large groups, you'll want a large cooking area—six burners at least. The best kind of grill surface is cast iron; the second best is stainless steel. Enamel is my least favorite because the grill marks you get aren't as good." A few other tips: "You want a good grease evaporation system, a built-in thermometer, and a built-in gas gauge—and you can never have too many side tables."

How to find out if the grill you like cooks as great as it looks? "I recommend that people go to a barbecue store—like Barbecues Galore (see Resources page 156)—where they fire up the grills on the weekend and try them out. Remember: Expensive doesn't always mean great. You can spend a lot of money on a poorly designed grill."

the indoor kitchen? Will the prep work—washing and cutting vegetables, cleaning meat and fish—take place outdoors, or primarily indoors? Do you like to have family and friends milling around you—possibly helping—as you cook, or do you prefer your own private workspace? The answers to these questions will help you plan the best layout for your outdoor kitchen.

Finally, think about when you'll be cooking outdoors—year-round, during warm and cool weather, or only a few months a year? During the day or at night? Your habits will guide you to the best location, structure, and lighting plan for your outdoor kitchen.

MAKE A LIST, CHECK IT TWICE

Now that you've considered what, how, and when you'll be cooking in your outdoor kitchen, it's time to get down to brass tacks—deciding exactly what to include in the new space. As with any design project, it's always a good practice to start with an idea folder. Fill the folder with pictures from magazines or books, photographs of friends' outdoor

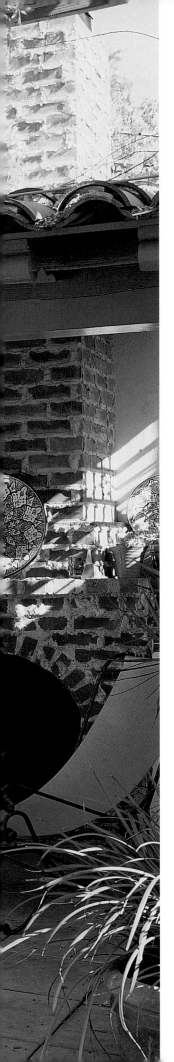

kitchens, product brochures from manufacturers, and the like. As you fill your file, don't be too discriminating. The goal is to assemble a wide-ranging trove of materials—some practical, some whimsical—that you can use to spark your imagination. As you flip through the images of table settings, grilling areas, landscaping plans, and so on, you'll start to see themes emerge—many spaces with a rustic look, say, or several high-tech setups. Once you've identified the look you like best, you can use that information, along with the cooking and entertaining habits you've already noted, to start your list of outdoor kitchen must-haves.

Your list should have several categories. Start with layout. You might write "near the dining room," for example, or "freestanding." Consider all the elements that will shape the space: size, location, adjacent areas such as a dining table or bar, and large features such as an island or built-in countertop. Next, move on to choosing the appliances. Let your cooking style guide you as you list the equipment you'll need: grill (Gas or charcoal? Barrel smoker? Rotisserie? See page 45 for descriptions of the various options), warming drawer, hood, refrigerator, dishwasher, sink, faucet—you get the picture. Materials should follow. You'll need to decide on surfacing if you're planning to incorporate a countertop into your plans, and paving if you'll be building the kitchen in a previously unpaved area. Don't forget to consider other integrated elements, such as lighting, heating (an outdoor fireplace?), and built-in furniture (a bench?), as well as large furniture items such as a dining set and umbrella. Finally, note where you'll need to run wires or pipes for electricity, water, and gas.

A PERFECT FIT

You can certainly spend whatever you want on an outdoor kitchen; it all depends on your budget, your needs (and wants), and your site. The good news is that even the smallest investment can give you a great return on your planning time—as long as you shop carefully. Some examples of what a budget, moderately priced, and no-holds-barred outdoor kitchen might look like follow.

Realizing the outdoor kitchen of your dreams depends in large part on the time you spend in the planning phase. Determine the elements you can't live without, as well as the extras that will make your workspace something special. Note the features that make this outdoor kitchen so inviting: a partial covering with Spanish-style tiles, a cozy brick hearth, and a casual dining area.

Even a fairly basic freestanding grill can give you an efficient workspace. Look for models that seem sturdy and that offer side tables and a concealed cabinet for the propane canister.

BASIC

A simple—but well-equipped—outdoor cooking area might include a moderately priced, freestanding gas grill, ideally with side tables and a side burner (if you find that the side burner on your grill isn't powerful enough, you might consider a separate propane-fueled burner of the type commonly used to boil large pots of water for cooking seafood), and a portable work surface, such as a rolling butcher-block-topped cart or table. Close proximity to the indoor kitchen cuts down on trips hauling heavy food and dishes, and a nearby dining area adds comfort and eases entertaining. Depending on how much you decide to spend on the grill—the average freestanding gas grill sells for about the same cost as a good microwave oven—you can manage a no-frills setup for about the same price as a quality indoor range.

MODERATE

In the middle of the price range you might find a basic built-in gas grill set into a custom-made grill island, available from a wide variety of sources, both prefinished and in do-it-yourself kit form. Grill islands start at about twice the cost of an indoor kitchen range, for a very small grill surround; prices go up according to size, materials, and

options—you can request a sink, heated interior drawers, and granite surfacing from some manufacturers. Don't forget to factor in the cost of features such as lighting and shelter to protect the island from the elements. Building a small countertop might cost less, depending on expenses for material and labor; but keep in mind that, though it's bulky, a premade self-contained grill island is actually portable—a nice feature in a cold climate.

SPLURGE

If you decide to go all out, well, the sky's the limit. You can spend thousands on the design alone (before you've set foot in the appliance showroom), then pile on professional-grade appliances such as an extra-large built-in grill, outdoor refrigerator, dishwasher, sink, faucet, warming drawer, stone surfacing, outdoor fireplace or pizza oven, lighting—the works. There's really no way to estimate costs for this category, but a high-end, feature-filled outdoor kitchen can easily cost as much as an indoor kitchen.

So, how much should you spend on your new kitchen? That depends, of course, on your bank account. But, rest assured, though there aren't figures on the cost versus resale value of installing an outdoor kitchen, outdoor living spaces always add to a home's worth—not to mention to the enjoyment of the people who live there. Most homeowners will probably settle on the happy medium of the moderate setup; and, with the right attitude, you can create a cooking space that's every bit as attractive and efficient as one with a designer price tag. But you'll need to pay close attention to the basic building blocks of design—location and layout—and you might do well to consult with a professional kitchen designer or landscape architect. Savvy shopping will help you find good deals on the equipment you really need and want. (Check end-of summer clearance sales.) The Internet is a great resource for bargains on every type of material; chances are, the more time you spend online, the less money you'll spend on your kitchen.

LOCATION IS EVERYTHING

Where you decide to build your outdoor kitchen will affect everything from the way you use the new workspace to the appearance of your home and landscaping—so proceed carefully. The most common placement for an outdoor kitchen is along a wall of the house, on an existing deck or patio. This type of location has many benefits: close proximity to indoor cooking areas and to electricity, water, and gas services from the house; shelter from the elements; and existing paving. However, before you settle on this most obvious spot, you'll

need to determine if it provides enough space for the features you have in mind. Most grills range from 24" (61 cm) to as much as 48" (122 cm) wide and 15" (38 cm) to 26" (66 cm) inches deep; side burners or tables add about 12" (30.5 cm) on either side. Plan at least 36" (91.5 cm) of counterspace on each side of the grill if possible, to allow a landing zone for hot foods, a prep area, and a serving station. Similarly, you should allow 18" (45.5 cm) to 24" (61 cm) of counterspace on either side of a sink. Are you planning to include a dining area in your outdoor living space? A square table for four is about 42" x 42" (106.5 x 106.5 cm); one that seats six to eight might be as long as 96" (244 cm). Ideally, you should allow 42" (106.5 cm) of space between the edge of the table and a wall or other structure, so there's room to push back chairs or walk behind those who are seated. And the table should be at least 60" (152.5 cm) from any staircase. Also, note factors such as light and wind patterns: You don't want to stand in front of a grill with the setting sun shining in your eyes, and your guests shouldn't have to chat through billowing smoke as they wait patiently for your famous fork-tender brisket.

FREESTANDING OR ATTACHED

One big decision concerning the location of the outdoor kitchen will be whether it should be attached to the house or freestanding. Both styles have benefits—and drawbacks—

A high-end outdoor kitchen can be a sizeable investment. But if you cook outdoors frequently, you'll enjoy the convenience of the amenities you've built into your workspace. And, if your budget is big enough, you'll find your options are nearly unlimited.

If you plan a freestanding kitchen, make sure that the design of the enclosure—should you build one—offers plenty of air circulation. The high roof and open sides of this design ensure that smoke does not get trapped inside.

and which you choose will depend on your lifestyle, budget, and site. An attached outdoor kitchen, as described earlier, has the advantage of close proximity to the indoor kitchen—a plus from a convenience standpoint, certainly, but also because it simplifies utility hookups—protection from the elements by the house itself, and, if there's an existing patio in place, a perfect foundation. However, if your back door opens onto a deck, you'll probably have to reinforce the deck before installing all but the most rudimentary outdoor cooking equipment. Attached outdoor kitchens are by their very nature defined by the existing site; you will have to base the size, shape, and style on the house and surrounding areas, so your options might be somewhat limited.

A freestanding kitchen, on the other hand, allows you a clean slate from a design perspective. If you've always

wanted a Polynesian grass hut (but live in a clapboard colonial), you can create your very own beach-style snack shack—and it won't look out of place as long as it's not too close to the house. Which brings up the first drawback of freestanding outdoor kitchens: They're usually not as convenient to the indoor kitchen, so it's best to make them self-contained, with storage, cooling, and cleanup right at hand. The second drawback is expense. You'll have to build a freestanding outdoor kitchen from scratch, incurring considerably more expense than if you built just a countertop or two along the wall of your house. Utility hookups are more complicated and expensive as well. Still, you can place the freestanding kitchen exactly where you want it—near a pool, say, facing a particularly beautiful view, away from prevailing winds—and outfit it for entertaining a large crowd, if you like.

THE RIGHT SITE

Choosing the best location for your kitchen means considering a wide variety of factors, such as topography, prevailing winds, weather, and safety. Let's start with topography. If you're blessed with a level site, you're all set. But if you're working with an uneven or sloping location, you'll have to amend it to ensure an adequate foundation and proper drainage. Here's where the services of a professional landscape architect can come in handy. Heavy winds can wreak havoc on your carefully laid plans, driving guests inside or spreading smoke from the barbecue across entertaining areas. One way to evaluate wind patterns in your chosen site is by planting several makeshift flags—stakes with a piece of fabric attached will work—around the area; then, watch to see how the flags move throughout the day. If the site seems too breezy, you may want to erect a windbreak nearby. A latticework fence or row of shrubs can do the trick nicely.

The climate in which you live, and the microclimates within your backyard, will also impact the way you experience your outdoor kitchen. In rainy areas, provide cover overhead; in excessively sunny spots, plan shade from trees, a ceiling or pergola overhead, or a retractable awning. Cold climates require more extensive planning (see page 117) to keep the outdoor kitchen comfortable. Finally, think long and hard about safety. Live-fire cooking can be dangerous unless proper precautions are taken. Keep open flames far from flammable structures, including roof overhangs, wooden fences, trees, and decks. All materials around the grill should be flame resistant, as well.

DESIGNING FOR THE WHOLE FAMILY

Outdoor entertaining areas are, more or less by definition, family-centered places with no fussy fabrics or furnishings to worry about and no delicate breakables to watch over. They're the ideal spot for kids to hang out, especially if they're anywhere near a pool. So it's essential that you keep kids in mind as you finalize your plan. And whenever kids are involved, safety is priority number one. Grilling is by its very nature a high-heat endeavor; it's imperative to take every possible step to keep kids away from the grill. Opting for a kitchen layout that blocks the grill from general family

For practical reasons, the location of your outdoor kitchen is key. Here, the kitchen is close to the house but is distinguished by its rustic wood-and-twig shelter.

traffic with an island or a run of cabinetry is your best bet (though, of course, a grill should never be left unattended when children are around). Eating areas—such as a snack bar or table—should be well separated from the cooking appliances, and kid magnets, such as soda-stocked refrigerators, should be placed carefully, as well. Consider installing the beverage center outside the kitchen proper to prevent children from straying too close to the work zone. Tools such as knives, matches, electric igniters, food processors, and even blenders should be kept out of sight and out of reach. Rounded corners on countertops and tables can prevent injuries, as can railings on even the shortest stairway.

Don't worry: Keeping a watch on safety during the planning stages will help you and your family relax and enjoy the new space once it's finished—and there's still plenty of room for fun. As you choose materials, look for bright colors that will appeal to the whole family. Let children in on the design process by taking them with you to appliance centers or tile showrooms, or by allowing them to choose a special kids' table or fun plastic plates and cups. The more your family is involved in the planning, the more they'll appreciate the great results.

SEEKING PROFESSIONAL HELP

If you envision a fairly extensive outdoor kitchen addition or if you're new to kitchen design, you might benefit from some professional assistance. A certified kitchen designer (though these professionals specialize in indoor kitchen design, many, especially in warm climates, have long experience in planning outdoor cooking and entertaining areas), a landscape architect, or an in-store designer at the local home center are all quite capable of helping you create your dream space. Fees vary widely by area and the scope of your project, but you're likely to find that hiring a professional may actually save you money in the long run by eliminating costly mistakes that can send your budget into overdrive. An expert will also help you evaluate the site, plan the most efficient layout for your cooking style, find the best deal on appliances and materials, and source unique design elements you'd probably never come across yourself.

How to find a designer? Often, your friends and family are the best resource—whenever you see an outdoor kitchen you like, ask who designed and installed it. Or, you can contact local or national professional associations (see Resources, page 156) to find design professionals in your area. Many association websites offer general design information, guidelines on hiring a pro, and even sample

Because an outdoor kitchen is usually a place where the whole family will gather, it makes sense to consider the kids during the design phase. Plan for safety, of course, but also provide some comfortable—and fun—hangout areas for little ones.

SHOULD YOU DO IT YOURSELF?

Completing some of the work yourself may help you save money on your outdoor kitchen, but before you grab your toolbox, take the time to evaluate your skill level. If you're a novice, you'll probably be happier with the results if you hire a professional contractor for jobs like building countertops and installing paving—or at least if you recruit an experienced friend to help and teach you. But if you have some carpentry or building experience, you'll find that with plenty of time and planning you can successfully build and install structures such as a grill island, arbor, or tiled countertop. See Chapter Seven: You Can Do It (page 141) for instructions on these three projects; your local home center will likely have information and plans for more extensive jobs.

ASK THE RIGHT QUESTIONS

As you meet with designers, landscape architects, and contractors, be sure to ask each one the same questions so that later you'll be able to compare "apples to apples." A few good queries follow:

- **Do you have a portfolio?** If possible, review before-and-after photographs. Choose someone whose previous work you admire.

- **Do you have any completed projects I can visit?** Sometimes, seeing the real thing can tell you a lot about the quality and detail of a professional's work.

- **Will you be my main contact during the project?** If you're not comfortable working with a team of assistants while the main professional oversees the job from afar, be sure to hire someone who will work with you for the duration of the project.

- **Are you fully licensed and insured?** Determining this status may be the key to avoiding litigation later.

- **Are you a member of any trade organization?** Certified Kitchen Designers (CKD) receive ongoing training and credentials from the National Kitchen & Bath Association (NKBA). Other trade organizations govern members with a code of business ethics.

- **Do you have a list of (checkable) references?** Never hire anyone who can't provide you with a list of previous satisfied clients. And don't neglect to call them!

- **What is your fee system?** Some professionals charge a flat fee; others may charge by the hour; others may charge a percentage of the total job up front.

TIPS OF THE TRADE

Can't afford to hire a pro to plan your outdoor kitchen? Follow these pointers and you might not need one:

1. Plan for perfection. Professionals spend more time planning a job than installing it. Take the time to consider every element of the kitchen. Sketch it on graph paper. Wait a week, and then look at the plan again. Time is an essential ingredient in any building project,

2. Do your research. A professional designer has all the facts at his or her fingertips. Research before beginning a job—make sure to find out about local codes and key features of your property (such as the location of the septic system and power lines) before you settle on a site.

3. Shop carefully. Professionals know from long experience which products perform well and which don't. You'll have to rely on word of mouth and product reviews, but if you take the time to do a background check on all appliances before you buy, you'll probably be a lot happier with your purchases in the long run. The Internet is the ideal shopping partner.

contracts. Before you hire anyone, however, make sure he or she understands your goals for the projects as well as your budget. Have several conversations to ensure a good rapport—on a large project, you may spend several months working with this person, so you should feel comfortable together. Insist on a detailed contract that spells out the progression of the work to be done (with dates) as well as all fees and payment schedules. Before you sign on the dotted line, take the time to carefully check references, insurance, and permits.

EVERYTHING IN ITS PLACE

Think about your indoor kitchen for a moment. Imagine yourself cooking there—preparing foods, taking things in and out of the refrigerator and cabinets, cooking, and cleaning up. As you work, you make hundreds of movements between appliances, work surfaces, the sink, and the trash receptacle. If your kitchen has an efficient layout, you never have to move far while completing a certain task. When you're preparing vegetables, for example, the refrigerator where they're stored, the sink where you'll wash them, the surface where you'll cut them, and even the trash can where you'll scrape the peels and discarded ends are all clustered together—you don't waste time walking back and forth across the room as you work. The outdoor kitchen should be just as carefully laid out, even though, in most spaces, its significantly smaller size will help eliminate unnecessary steps.

If you're happy with the design of your indoor kitchen, you might translate its features to the outdoor cooking space, albeit on a smaller scale. For example, if you love pivoting between your perimeter countertops and a central island inside, you might plan a small island (or even a rolling cart or table) opposite the grilling center outside. If you work well with a peninsula counter inside, you might opt to design one outside.

Working with a professional designer can help you integrate your new outdoor kitchen into the architecture of your house as well as into your landscaping plan. A functional design might include a small grill island—either custom-built or prefabricated—and a built-in grill set at the edge of an existing patio or deck.

Planning the layout of your outdoor kitchen needn't be complicated. An efficient workspace can be as simple—and as beautiful— as this small counter tucked into a flower-draped trellis. Cabinets hide propane tanks and provide storage.

GEOMETRY FOR THE OUTDOOR KITCHEN

If you'd like to incorporate the principle of the work triangle into your outdoor kitchen, keep in mind the following guidelines from the NKBA. Note that many outdoor kitchens will be fairly small; these measurements apply best to larger spaces.

- Each leg of the triangle should be between 4' (1.2 m) and 9' (2.7 m) long.
- The total length of all three sides should fall between 12' (3.7 m) and 26' (7.9 m).
- General traffic patterns should not interfere with the work triangle.
- Cabinetry should not intersect any triangle leg by more than 12" (30.5 cm).

Of course, more important than the shape of your outdoor kitchen or whether it's designed with the work triangle in mind is how the layout works for you. A short run of counterspace with a grill toward one end, a sink toward the other, and an outdoor refrigerator someplace in the middle can function with perfect efficiency. What should really determine the layout of your cooking space is how you intend to use it, so consider the following questions: How many people will use the space at one time? One or two, or a crowd? And what will each person be doing? Cooking at the same time—say one at the grill, the other at a wok—or will one person stick to prep while the other tends the fire? Will there be children around? (See page 69 for information on how to plan a safe outdoor kitchen.) Will you have onlookers? Where will they sit? Do you want them in the cooking area at all? What kind of space do you need to allot for comfortable passage between the outdoor kitchen and other outdoor features such as doors to the house, seating areas, pool, and so on? How many appliances will you include? How much room do they take up? (Don't forget to allow room for refrigerator doors to open.) And how much space is needed for cabinetry? These questions, and others that will occur to you as you evaluate your needs, will help you come up with a layout that's right for your unique cooking style and site.

PLAN FOR SUCCESS

If your outdoor kitchen will be attached to one of the exterior walls of your house, you'll probably find yourself settling on one of three layout styles: straight, modified galley, or L-shape (see pages 30–31 for illustrated examples). A straight layout is the easiest to arrange and least expensive to build; the main goal is to ensure that you'll have enough room to work comfortably and safely.

Outdoors, a galley layout usually takes the form of a countertop along one wall with an island or other work surface directly opposite it. The benefits of this plan are several: The island provides an extra surface for food prep, storage, and even seating; it also provides a buffer between the general flow of traffic and the cook. Depending on your setup, the island might house a sink or refrigerator, or even the grill—which gives the advantage of allowing the cook to face out toward the surrounding patio—or it might just function as another countertop.

An L-shape layout is basically a run of cabinets and countertop with a return at one end. This setup is a good way to maximize a small cooking space; the return doesn't require as much room as an island and may take the place of a separate dining table if you design it accordingly. The disadvantage of an L-shape layout outside is that it leaves the cooking area open to traffic and keeps the cook's back to the crowd.

If you envision a large, fully equipped outdoor cooking space—particularly if it will be freestanding—you should also consider the U-shape and G-shape layouts. The U-shape is enclosed on three sides, allowing appliance placement in a neat, compact triangle—an efficient arrangement that saves steps for the cook. One side remains open, providing a nice link to adjoining spaces, so that the cook feels connected to guests. The G-shape layout is similar, except that it provides a fourth work surface. The extra amenities the U- and G-shape plans allow make them ideal for those who plan to entertain frequently—you'll have no problem fitting in extras such as warming drawers and an ice maker.

Whichever layout you choose, keep in mind that the whole point of an outdoor kitchen is to enjoy the outdoors, so make sure it won't feel too enclosed. The sides of the kitchen should be open, even if it's under cover from the elements, and an easy flow should exist between cooking and relaxation areas. It's always smart to plan for more storage than you could ever imagine needing and to consider ways to hide unsightly messes (dishes and leftover marinade, for example) from sight while you eat. You might keep an undercounter shelf open so you can stash dirty plates until you're ready to carry them inside, or plan a dual-level island or countertop so that the "work" portion of the counter is hidden from sight by a higher level closest to the dining or lounging area. Serving the meals you cook outdoors is as important to the process as preparation, so be sure to allow an open area to place dishes before carrying them to the table, or even to set up a self-serve buffet.

FOCUS ON: THE WORK TRIANGLE

What exactly is the work triangle? Simply put, it's a layout tool that kitchen designers have been using since the 1950s to create an efficient kitchen floor plan. The triangle represents the flow between the three major work centers: the sink, the cooking surface, and the refrigerator. When well implemented, the work triangle saves the cook not only steps but time. Should you consider the work triangle when designing your outdoor kitchen? Experts' opinions differ—partially because outdoor kitchens often consist of a single run of appliances with counterspace in between—but most agree that if you're planning a large, fully outfitted outdoor kitchen, using the triangle concept still makes good design sense. To get an idea of how the kitchen triangle works, take a look at the four most common kitchen layouts:

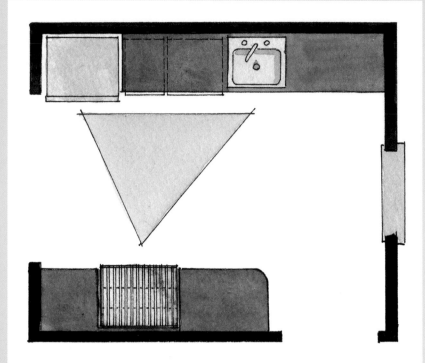

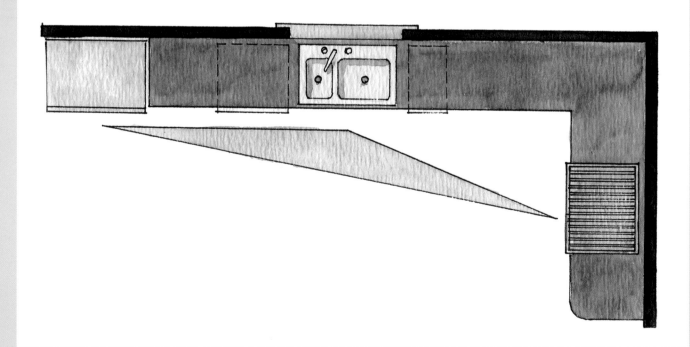

▲ (TOP) *GALLEY SHAPE* In this type of space, the major kitchen elements are directly opposite each other. Indoors, they're located on opposite walls; outside, a galley might consist of appliances against one wall and a sink set into a facing island.

▲ (ABOVE) *L-SHAPE* Building an L-shape counter creates a natural work triangle and allows plenty of room for meal preparation and serving, or even a small snack bar.

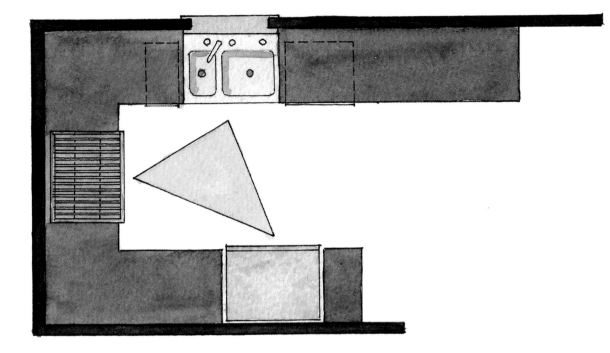

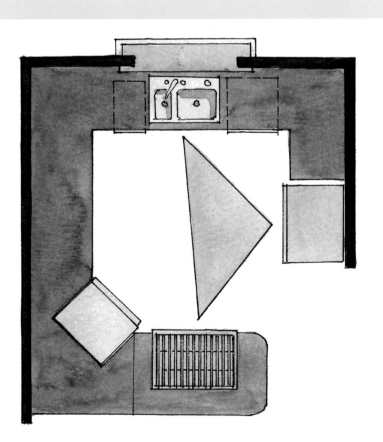

▲ **U-SHAPE** *Appropriate for larger, more completely outfitted outdoor kitchens, a U-shape layout surrounds the cook with appliances and prep surfaces on three sides.*

◄ **G-SHAPE** *Outdoors, this layout is usually used only for a freestanding kitchen; it effectively reproduces the plan of an indoor kitchen—providing an entire "room" for the dedicated outdoor chef.*

ADVANCED PLACEMENT

Once you've determined the basic layout of your cooking space, you'll need to decide where each element should go, starting with the appliances. If yours will be a simple outdoor kitchen, this part will be easy: Place the grill toward one end of a built-in counter or grill island, leaving open areas of countertop on each side, one larger than the other. This placement will give you a small space to set tools and marinades while you work as well as another space for finished dishes and prep work. If, on the other hand, you'll be including several appliances in your kitchen, the right placement for each element will depend on how you plan to use them.

Imagine yourself working in the new space. What happens first? Prep work? If so, set up a sink, counter, and refrigerator cluster in one area. This zone will double as the cleanup center, so if a dishwasher figures into your plans, place it near the sink. Next, group cooking features in another spot, slightly separated from the prep zone. Arrange the cooking appliances according to your own habits. If you're left-handed, for instance, a separate side burner or wok ring should be to the left of the grill, so you can give a stir-fry pan a shake with your left hand while standing in front of the grill. Any features you plan to use only occasionally—a charcoal kettle grill, say, or a ceramic Kamado-style cooker—should be accessible but out of the way of everyday cooking.

WORKING TOGETHER

As you sketch your new outdoor kitchen on graph paper and stuff pictures into your idea file, it can be easy to forget that the space will not exist in a vacuum. On the contrary, it will be a part of a hardscaping plan that includes a wide variety of permanent features, such as your house, existing patios or decks, walkways, stairways, railings, fences, pool, pool house, and garden structures, such as a pergola or arbor. So unless the kitchen will be freestanding and completely hidden from view of the main house, you should plan its scale and style with a nod to the architectural flavor of the elements that will surround it.

An L-shape kitchen layout like this one gives the cook more room to spread out equipment and perform prep work such as chopping and cleaning vegetables, yet still keeps the cooking area open to surrounding lounging spaces.

A straight run of countertop isn't just for small kitchen spaces. It's an efficient plan that many cooks find works best for them in any setting. The longer the run of countertop and cabinets, the more room for multiple cooks to work in tandem.

DWAYNE RIDGAWAY

Though he lives in Rhode Island, chef and cookbook author Dwayne Ridgaway was raised in Texas, and he has an admitted soft spot for barbecue—despite the fact that these days he's more likely to cook pizza on the grill than a slow-basted brisket. Ridgaway honed his cooking—and grilling—skills as the chef at numerous resorts and restaurants, including the San Destin Beach Resort and the Elephant Walk in Florida, and as the author of several cookbooks, including *Lasagna, Sandwiches, Panini, and Wraps,* and his latest, *Indoor Grilling* (all for Quarry Books). Today, Ridgaway is a food and beverage consultant and caterer with some great, practical tips for homeowners setting up an outdoor cooking area.

Professional Help

"In the summer, I probably cook more outside than I do inside," says Ridgaway. "Anything's appropriate for the grill," he adds. "Steak, fish, chicken—and I do a lot of grilled pizzas." To get the bold grill marks on his creations, Ridgaway prefers to use a charcoal grill with a sturdy, heavyweight cooking grate, though he also uses a gas grill from time to time.

As many homeowners have chosen, Ridgaway's outdoor kitchen is in close proximity to his indoor workspace. "I have a deck right off my kitchen that has a marble countertop and a glass-topped dining table; then it's only steps down to a patio that has more lounge-style seating." But while he has a fairly large cooking and entertaining area, the chef notes that space footage is not a requirement for an attractive, efficient outdoor kitchen. "You need to think about the functionality of the space and the flow before you buy anything," he says. "A lot of people—probably guys, especially—want to buy these huge grills that take up 75 percent of their space, and you shouldn't do that. Only buy what you need."

Another useful tip from Ridgaway: Be creative. "I like to use things in unexpected ways. My counter is a huge slab of marble that I attached to the side of the house with brackets, then supported in front with turned columns from the porch of a house being torn down in my neighborhood." His dining table is a piece of glass set atop two marble balustrades originally from the balcony of another tear-down. "It can be overwhelming to create an outdoor kitchen from scratch—it's a big investment—so think about using what you already have, just in a new way."

In fact, if the kitchen will be connected to the house, it can provide a neat transition from interior living areas to outdoor lounging spaces. The easiest way to achieve this is by using "outdoor" materials for its structure—a pergola or arbor hung with vines for the overhead shelter, for instance, and island facing and countertop surfacing that occurs elsewhere outdoors—the same tile on the backsplash that borders the inside of the swimming pool, say, or stucco on the sides of the grill island in the same shade as that on the exterior walls of the house. And just as you've planned a close relationship between the indoor and outdoor kitchen, you should consider proximity to other key comfort spaces, such as a bathroom, mudroom, or pool house, if you have one; you'll enjoy cooking outside more if you don't have to go far for supplies like extra paper napkins or another bag of charcoal.

FINE DINING

Because one main function of an outdoor kitchen is to allow you to spend more time outside, the most successful cooking spaces work in close symbiosis with a dining area. We'll talk more about designing a comfortable, stylish dining area in chapter three, but it's smart to think about how the two spaces will relate to each other while you're still in the design phase of the project. For example, do you want the cooking center to be open to the dining area, or would you

HOT TIPS

Landscape designer Michael Glassman, principal of Michael Glassman & Associates, a landscape design and consultation firm in Sacramento, California, says that although several years ago few clients asked for outdoor kitchens, today they're almost a prerequisite. His advice for homeowners follows:

• **Plan ahead.** "It's really crucial that you run a gas line, plumbing, and a dedicated circuit and electrical line for the outdoor kitchen, even if you're planning to build it in stages. Otherwise, you'll just have to jackhammer up the patio or run unnecessarily long electrical lines later."

• **Choose materials carefully.** "I want the outdoor kitchens I design to be an integral part of the landscaping design as a whole, so if we've previously done planters of plastered concrete block, for example, we'll build the cooking center out of concrete block and plaster it. I also try to coordinate indoor and outdoor spaces, so I might use the same granite for outdoor countertops as on indoor surfaces."

• **Site it right.** "Today, the trend is for everyone to gather around the cooking area—the cooking is part of the 'activity' of a party. So plan an outdoor bar where people can sit and a serving area where you can set up salads or drinks."

• **Provide shade.** "People want to cook and sit outdoors without burning up, so plan some sort of overhead structure, whether it's a trellis or something solid."

A dining area should be comfortable and inviting. The built-in fireplace gives this sheltered living space an inviting warmth, perfect for chilly summer evenings.

In a compact outdoor kitchen, appliance placement is simple. Just be sure to leave yourself a landing pad for utensils and plates on either side of the grill.

rather have a buffer between the cook and the diners? Think about a restaurant with an open kitchen; the preparation of the food becomes part of the entertainment, and the chef is the star of the show. If this kind of role appeals to you, keep the kitchen in close sight of the dining area. But if the watchful eyes of hungry guests make you feel flustered as you try to put the finishing touches on a gourmet meal, you might appreciate some visual distance between work and play areas. How you and your family and friends will eat outside impacts the design of the cooking area as well. Casual family meals may require simply the addition of a table and six chairs to your scheme—or just a snack bar at the end of the outdoor kitchen counter; but serving larger

numbers, or entertaining with a formal atmosphere, will call for a more carefully orchestrated dining area.

If you do plan to entertain large groups, at least occasionally, it's certainly a good idea to include a capacious island or a long, open countertop in your kitchen layout. This setup will provide a nice big area for hors d'oeuvres trays, a casual buffet, or a staging station for caterers. In addition, features you might not need when cooking just for the family can come in handy when entertaining a crowd: Consider a second sink for mixing cocktails—or a dedicated cocktail bar, even—warming drawers for keeping multiple courses or hot appetizers at the perfect temperature, a beverage refrigerator and an ice maker, and, of course, a grill with an extra-large cooking surface. Storage should include room for serving trays. As you lay out the kitchen and surrounding spaces, plan for expansion: an open side yard near the kitchen will accommodate a tent for large parties, lounge chairs can be moved out of the way for a row of rented dining tables. Outdoor lighting should illuminate all pathways and stairways in addition to highlighting attractive features of your garden, patio, and house.

Outside, landscaping elements are your true decorating tools. By integrating your landscape and hardscape, you'll give your outdoor kitchen a pretty, natural feel.

NATURAL BEAUTY

Just as the design of an outdoor kitchen should work in concert with surrounding hardscaping elements, it should also reflect a careful consideration of landscaping features. First, consider the big picture. What's around the future kitchen site? Are there any great views you'd like to maximize (or not-so-great views you'd prefer to screen)? Should the shape of the kitchen mimic a theme of the landscaping; for example, if you have a curving garden border, it might be pleasing to plan a curving run of cabinetry and countertop. A kitchen space with a traditional design will complement a formal landscaping plan, whereas a rustic-looking workspace will look right at home in relationship to a desert or mountainside backdrop.

Next, shift into sharp focus by examining the areas in immediate proximity to the new kitchen and planning accordingly. The scale of the space should be in keeping with significant nearby plantings, and the shape can balance existing trees, shrubs, or borders. The style of the kitchen can gain much from plantings in a similar vein; an outdoor living space with an exotic flair looks particularly well coordinated when paired with plantings that have a tropical look or an Asian feel—think of a stand of bamboo near the edge of a Zen-inspired seating area. Open kitchen shelters, such as a pergola overhead or latticework "walls," lend greater cover and privacy when planted with vines—grapes above, perhaps, and clematis or roses on the vertical surfaces. Choose species with fragrant flowers to delight guests relaxing in nearby dining and lounging areas and herbs you can use as you cook.

PRACTICAL MATTERS

Though it's more fun to think about how many BTUs (British thermal units, a measure of heat) your new grill will boast or which tiles to install along the backsplash, none of your fabulous plans will mean a thing if you don't pay just as much attention to certain nitty-gritty details—plumbing, for one. If you'd like a sink in your outdoor kitchen, you'll have to provide it with water somehow. That means running a line from the house—which is simple if the kitchen is connected to the house, but more complex (and expensive) if it's some distance away. If you live in a cold climate, the water line will have to be buried beneath

Don't forget your own comfort as you choose the elements for your kitchen. Plan some sort of protection from the sun—like this cheery orange umbrella—and, if necessary, a wind screen.

CODES AND PERMITS

There is no national code regulating outdoor kitchen or grill construction. However, some municipalities do have standards regarding where you can have an open fire and how close to lot lines you can build. Protect your project—and your pocketbook—by taking the time to contact your local planning board to research local codes and zoning regulations in your area. You may need to obtain construction permits as well, particularly if the project includes plumbing or electrical work. If you're working with a licensed contractor or architect, he or she may be able to obtain these permits for you.

frost level, insulated, and, in some cases, fitted with a heated wire wrap at the point it leaves the ground to connect to the sink. Alternatively, you might opt for a shut-off valve inside the house so you can easily drain the pipes in the winter. Or, just hook a garden hose to the sink, making sure to run it neatly out of sight, perhaps hidden by some low shrubs, and disconnect it when the weather turns cold. (For more on plumbing and drainage, see page 53.)

Fuel is another important consideration. Gas grills run on propane or natural gas—either of which must be piped from your main tank or line (though many gas grills can also use separate, self-contained propane canisters). And you'll also need electricity for lighting, for appliances such as a refrigerator or warming drawer, and for accessories such as a blender or food processor. The main safety concern here is protecting the electrical ground path (so that it doesn't accidentally flow into conductors like metal appliances). Circuits should be grounded, and ground fault circuit interrupters (GCFIs) must be installed for extra protection. Unless you're an experienced hand in plumbing and electrical work and are aware of local building codes and needed permits, it's a good idea to hire a licensed professional for all utility connections.

CHAPTER TWO

THE RIGHT STUFF
OUTFITTING YOUR OUTDOOR KITCHEN

Now that you have a good sense of the style, location, and layout of your outdoor kitchen, it's time to fire up your budget and start shopping. You'll soon find that hundreds of different grills are available—not to mention smokers, rotisseries, pizza ovens, and more—at price points from a few hundred to many thousands of dollars.

WHAT'S COOKING?

Because the grill is usually the centerpiece of any outdoor kitchen, this appliance is the best place to start. First, you'll need to decide whether you want a gas grill or a charcoal-burning unit (or both). Each type has its merits (and fans who'd never stoop to eating a burger cooked on one or the other kind). Gas grills—fueled by a portable tank of liquid propane or piped-in natural or propane gas—are convenient, offering push-button ignition, quick preheating, and no fires to stoke or ashes to empty. It's as easy to control the flame level as turning a knob, and many models even feature a built-in temperature gauge. However, gas grills are not ideal for true slow-cooked barbecue. Although newer models do have smoker trays in which you can place hardwood chips to create a smoky flavor, aficionados prefer charcoal grills for authentic barbecue results.

Charcoal grills burn hotter than their gas-fueled counterparts, and you can burn wood in a charcoal grill, imparting a bolder, smokier flavor to your food. But, they're messy—you have to remove the ashes each time you cook; the results are less predictable than those of gas grills; charcoal grills take longer to preheat; and they require restoking every hour because the coals lose heat.

Today's outdoor kitchens are often as feature-filled as their indoor counterparts, with professional-style grills, refrigerators, sinks, and storage. Not just valuable for its sleek good looks, stainless steel withstands rust and corrosion better than many other materials. It's definitely the best choice if your kitchen will be near the shore.

High-end, built-in gas grills offer a large grilling surface, high BTU output, sturdy stainless steel construction, and a host of extras including a rotisserie and even built-in lighting. Many manufacturers offer storage units as well.

Each type has its pluses and minuses, so which should you choose? For everyday grilling, a gas grill is probably your best bet: They're easy to use and come with a vast range of optional accessories. But for true barbecue flavor and the thrill of working with fire, invest in a charcoal grill, even if you use it only on occasional weekends. Electric grills are another option and may be the only choice for apartment or condo dwellers; they're convenient, but they don't impart a real barbecue flavor.

BUYING A GAS GRILL

Gas grills come in many shapes and sizes, can be free-standing or built-in, and cost anywhere from what you'd spend for a food processor to as much as you'd spend for a restaurant-grade kitchen range. Your cooking style, budget, and the site and layout of your outdoor kitchen will determine exactly which features you choose, but you should follow some general guidelines when evaluating gas grills.

First, the grill should look and feel sturdy and solid. All moving parts should move smoothly, and the drip pan should be easy to empty and clean. Second, the material it's made of should hold up to years of use. Grills are made from various materials: cast aluminum, sheet metal, cast iron, or stainless steel. Stainless steel is the best—and most expensive—choice because it withstands the elements best (although over time even stainless steel will degrade under

Although true smoking is best done on a charcoal grill, some gas grills have smoking chambers that you can fill with hardwood chips for imparting a smoky flavor to foods.

seaside conditions). Before you pay a premium for a stainless steel grill, make sure the frame of the grill is also stainless steel—some so-called stainless steel grills sit on a painted steel frame that may rust. Third, consider the fire power of the grill. You'll soon find that each grill has a different BTU rating. Note that having higher BTUs does not necessarily mean it's a hotter grill. You need to factor in the size of the grill and how well it maintains and distributes the heat—a smaller grill with a lower BTU rating might actually produce more heat.

Next, look at size. If you're planning to cook for a crowd, you'll want a large grate area with multiple burners; a smaller surface with, say, three burners is fine for meals for a family of four. Finally, the features should suit your needs. Look for a grill with at least two separately controlled burners, so that you can grill foods indirectly (this is the technique of choice for cooking larger items such as whole chickens), and two grate levels, that so you can keep some items warm while others finish cooking. A built-in temperature gauge will help you control the heat more precisely, and a gas gauge will keep you from running out of fuel in

WHAT PRICE, GREATNESS?

So what's the difference between a bargain-basement gas grill and an expensive high-end one? In truth, you can produce fantastic—or mediocre—results on just about any grill; the grill is just one of your tools as a cook. Still, factors such as construction, size, features, and warranty make some grills more expensive than others. A breakdown follows:

INEXPENSIVE MODELS (top)

The average gas grill sold today is in about the same price range as low- to high-priced microwave ovens. Lower-priced grills are usually smaller, with about 500 square inches (1270 cm²) of cooking space and an output of around 40,000 BTUs or fewer and are made from enameled steel or cast aluminum, with porcelain-coated or chrome-plated steel grates. The least expensive grills generally have the shortest lifespan—about five to ten years with proper care (regular cleaning and keeping the grill covered when not in use). You may have to replace the burners at some point during this time; if kept covered, the exterior should hold up quite well.

MID-RANGE GRILLS (center)

As the price of a grill goes up, so does the size, BTU rating, and quality of construction. Most grills in the middle price range have an output higher than 40,000 BTUs and multiple burners. With proper care, grills in this price range should last for at least ten years and will deliver good, consistent performance—but not many extras.

HIGH-END GRILLS (bottom)

High-end grills, which range in price from what you'd pay for a kitchen range to as much as ten times more, are designed for professional performance. They're often solid, high-gauge stainless steel from top to bottom, have large cooking surfaces, outputs of more than 50,000 BTUs, and come standard with many accessories such as powerful side burners, smoker trays, storage compartments, rotisseries, and even built-in lighting. Some feature infrared burners—long the standard in steak houses—which can reach temperatures of 1,000°F (538°C), ideal for searing meat. Warranties are higher, too; a grill in this price range should last a lifetime.

the middle of a family cookout. Accessories such as a smoker box or rotisserie can be nice, and on a freestanding grill, side burners, side tables, and even a small storage cabinet below the add convenience.

BUYING A CHARCOAL GRILL

For purists, when it comes to cooking outside, charcoal is the only way to go. After all, food cooked over a real wood fire has an intense smoky flavor, and true barbecue can be prepared only on a charcoal grill or smoker. A number of different types of charcoal grills and barbecues are available, but let's start with some basics. First, though the two terms are often used interchangeably, there's a big difference between "grilling" and "barbecuing." Grilling—cooking foods quickly, directly over high heat— is best for small, thin cuts of meat such as steaks or chops. True barbecuing, on the other hand, is a long, slow, low- heat process better suited to large cuts, such as brisket; the heat source is off to the side—sometimes removed from the cooking chamber entirely—and the food is cooked by indirect heat and smoke, often over the course of many hours. Here's a look at the most popular charcoal cooking options.

KETTLE GRILL

Invented in 1951 by George Stephen, the founder of the Weber-Stephen company, the kettle grill revolutionized grilling styles in America. Before Stephen's radical rethink, backyard cooking took place on a flat, brazier-style grill that was often built in, but because it was without a cover, it was little use in rainy or windy weather. Stephen, a barbecue aficionado and an employee at the Weber Brothers Metal Works, conceived of a spherical grill with a cooking grate set into a bowl and covered by a domed lid—and the iconic Weber Kettle Grill was born. The covered design makes it possible to use the indirect grilling method in a standard charcoal grill (see page 53); air vents at the top and bottom allow the cook to control the airflow—and therefore the temperature—inside.

BUILT-IN GRILL

Distant cousins of the flat brazier-style barbecues ubiquitous to suburban backyards in the 1950s and '60s, today's built-in grills are usually constructed of high-grade steel, with a hinged lid (which makes indirect grilling possible), air vents for temperature control, and easy ash-removal systems.

TABLE GRILL

Popular in Australia and Argentina, and with caterers, these grills have four legs and a flat, open grilling surface. They're ideal for cooking a large number of steaks or burgers but are not commonly used by homeowners.

HIBACHI

This portable Japanese grill is as simple as it is effective, consisting of a metal grate over a rectangular or oval fire- box, usually constructed of cast iron. The cook controls the temperature and cooking time by opening or closing vents at the bottom or by raising or lowering the grate. Hibachis are best for small, thin cuts of meats, kebabs, and satays.

If you want to cook authentic barbecued meats, you'll want an offset barrel smoker, or "pit." It has an offset firebox, so you can smoke a large amount of meat in the smoking chamber.

Based on an ancient Asian design, today's Kamado-style cookers are made from high-tech ceramic materials that can safely reach extremely high temperatures, or maintain the low temperatures ideal for slow smoking.

OTHER OPTIONS

You can smoke foods on most types of charcoal grill, but if you're a real barbecue aficionado you may want to supplement your grill with some kind of smoker. A few popular styles follow:

OFFSET BARREL SMOKER

Also called a "pit" and popular on the professional barbecue circuit (as well as in backyards across America), an offset smoker has a large, sometimes barrel-shaped smoking chamber and a separate firebox set off to the side. The large size of the cooking chamber allows you to cook hefty cuts of meat, such as a side of ribs or a whole pig, at a low temperature for a long period of time, until the meat is fall-off-the-bone tender and infused with a distinctive smoky-sweet flavor.

WATER SMOKER

A water smoker differs from a wood smoker in a number of ways. The smoker is arranged vertically, not horizontally, with the heat source at the bottom (either electric or charcoal), above which is a chamber for wood chips, a water chamber, and then finally a multilevel cooking chamber. As the fire heats the water, it boils, releasing steam into the air inside the smoker; the steam mixes with the smoke from the chips and creates a moist, smoky, perpetual basting effect. Water smoking is a long, slow process, but it's easier to maintain the low temperature on this type of unit than on a wood smoker, and the compact design and optional electric power source makes them a great choice for anyone with a small outdoor cooking space.

CERAMIC COOKERS

A modern adaptation of a 3,000-year-old tradition and first found in China, ceramic cooking was imported to Japan in

This electric grill is ideal for small spaces or anywhere you can't use a live-fire grill. And with 200 square inches (508 cm²) of cooking space, you can still cook for a crowd.

Many manufacturers offer a range of accessories. A rotisserie is probably the most popular grill attachment, because it allows you to grill a whole chicken perfectly evenly.

The former is first and foremost an appliance designed to extend the capabilities of your outdoor repertoire to include baked and roasted foods, whereas the latter can become an aesthetic element, just like a wood-burning hearth.

Wood-burning ovens are by their very nature custom features; you can start with a kit, but how you finish it is your choice. Popular finish materials include brick, stone, stucco, or tile; which you choose will impact the already-high price of the unit. Wood-burning ovens start at about the same price as a high-end grill, not including installation. If you don't plan to bake or roast outdoors, you still might appreciate the convenience of a warming drawer when it comes time to pull together a multicourse meal.

the form of the Kamado cooker. Today's ceramic cookers use high-tech ceramic materials to produce a combination grill, smoker, and oven that can cook at very high or very low temperatures while using a small amount of charcoal. Air vents allow you to control the temperature, and a porcelain outer coating keeps the surface much cooler to the touch than a metal grill—a nice feature when there are small children in the vicinity.

ELECTRIC GRILLS

If you live someplace where you can't use a charcoal or gas grill, you'll find numerous electric grills on the market. Purists will argue that the flavor these grills impart is a far cry from the real thing, but with ceramic briquettes and a rich marinade you probably won't notice the difference.

OUTDOOR OVENS

If you've decided to go above and beyond a basic outdoor kitchen setup, one helpful addition to your appliance plan is an oven or warming drawer. Ovens come in several forms but fall into two basic categories: gas or electric (much like your indoor oven, though some outdoor models offer unusual features like a smoking function) or a rustic wood-fired oven (of the sort used for baking pizza or bread).

Even if your outdoor space is limited to a small patio or balcony, you can still get true grilled flavor with an electric grill or a smoker.

A warming drawer will keep plates warm at its lowest setting, or turn it up to keep a stew steaming hot. Most have vents that you can adjust depending on whether the food to be warmed should be crispy or moist.

ACCESSORIZE

In addition to the wide range of grill types and sizes, you'll also find a dizzying array of grill accessories available. Which—if any—you choose will depend on your cooking style and your budget. Here's a look at a few of the most popular.

SIDE BURNER

If you're a dedicated outdoor cook, you'll find that a side burner is indispensable for preparing an entire meal outside. Without it, for example, you won't be able to cook rice to serve with your kebabs or boil corn to accompany your beer-can chicken. Even inexpensive gas grills often come equipped with a side burner—but beware: These burners are often barely powerful enough to simmer a saucepan of water, let alone boil a big pot of lobsters. If your budget is low, buy a separate propane-powered burner of the type often used for seafood boils (see Resources, page 156). High-end grills have high-powered side burners to match.

SIDE TABLES

Freestanding grills sometimes come with side tables you can flip up or down as needed. These features are a good option for space- or budget-challenged kitchens, but a work table or countertop is even better.

ROTISSERIE

A rotisserie makes it easy to cook perfectly browned birds or whole roasts on your grill. If the rotisserie is hooked up to a power source, the process is nearly effortless.

A built-in oven is a great addition to a full-featured outdoor kitchen. Use it to keep just-grilled foods warm, to bake bread or pizza, or to roast vegetables to serve on the side.

OFF

OVEN

OFF

Outdoor Electric
Smoker Oven

ON

LOW
200
250
300
400

TEMPERATURE

SMOKER

A high-output burner with a wok ring is a popular accessory. The high heat allows you to cook vegetables and meat quickly, and the ring keeps the wok steady and close to the flame.

WOK BURNER

If you're a fan of stir-fries, consider adding a high-output (more than 25,000 BTUs) wok burner to your setup. Or, buy a wok ring—a stainless steel ring that positions a wok properly on a regular burner.

CLEARING THE AIR

Though it might seem counterintuitive, proper ventilation is as important outdoors as it is inside. If your cooking space will be attached to your house or under any kind of shelter, it's crucial to factor a range hood into your plans. A large, commercial-grade hood will whisk away smoke, cooking odors, and grease, preventing it from wafting into nearby dining and conversation areas. Because it's difficult to accurately predict wind patterns when positioning a cooking area, even freestanding outdoor kitchens benefit from the addition of a range hood. Remember, the cook should be as comfortable as the guests, and you won't be if your eyes are stinging with smoke.

In addition to their powerful venting capacity, many units come with extras such as halogen lighting—always a nice feature when cooking outside at night—and hooks from which to hang utensils. Most hoods designed for outdoor use are stainless steel, which withstands abuse from the elements particularly well, but custom designs are also available. A custom hood is crafted from a ventilation insert that is then finished outside to fit your needs. You might opt for a wood facing (in a covered area) or a stucco or tiled design.

CLEANING UP

When the time comes to clean up your indoor kitchen, you probably don't give your sink and dishwasher a second thought—they're necessities, and you couldn't get along (happily) without them. But, whereas these two features are certainly essential indoors, they add considerable complexity and expense to an outdoor kitchen plan.

SINKING FEELING

A sink and running water add a huge amount of function and convenience to the outdoor kitchen. Even if you run only a cold-water line (the most popular approach), you'll still be able to wash dishes, fill pots, and rinse plates after the meal. Nonetheless, you'll have to consider several factors before deciding to install a sink. First, how will you feed the faucet? Some people run a cold-water line from the house. In cold climates, this line may have to be buried beneath the frost level, heavily insulated, and even heated with a wire wrap where it leaves the ground to meet the faucet. Others just use a garden hose—a particularly good option if you can keep it out of sight—that they can disconnect in the winter. Another option is to install a

line with an indoor valve so you can drain it before the start of cold weather each winter. In any case, you'll need to plan for drainage of waste water. You may be able to access your home's main drainage system and in a few cases an open drainage line may be possible, but many municipalities do not allow this (and few sites are well suited to this type of drainage, anyway). Alternatively, check with your municipality. If waste water is allowed, place a portable gray-water reservoir inside a cabinet underneath your sink. You'll need to empty it frequently, but if you avoid harsh soaps and chemicals you can use the gray water to water your flower beds.

Once you've gotten the logistics under control, choosing the sink and faucet is the easy part. Most outdoor kitchens have room for only a small sink, but fortunately even a bar sink is big enough to wash vegetables and rinse plates. If your outdoor kitchen is roomier, consider a sink large and deep enough for a commercial-style pot or roasting pan. The faucet should coordinate with the style of the sink: a delicate gooseneck for a small bar sink, a high-arcing pull-out faucet for a large, hardworking basin. Stainless steel is your best bet for both sink and faucet, unless the kitchen is completely covered, in which case, you'll find an endless range of styles and finishes.

GEORGE HIRSH

The author of five best-selling cookbooks, chef George Hirsch traces his love of food to his mother and Italian grandmother. From those earliest family influences, Hirsch's passion for cooking took him to the prestigious Culinary Institute of America, from which he graduated with high honors, and beyond—he is a Certified Executive Chef and a Culinary Educator and has been inducted into the Academy of Chefs by the American Culinary Federation. Today, he is perhaps best known for his show, *Living It Up!*, a public television series that emphasizes a healthy, active lifestyle.

Professional Help

George Hirsch is going on his third outdoor kitchen, so he knows a thing or two about how to design one. "My outdoor kitchen is really multipurpose," he says. "It's used for entertaining, but it's also used for the opening and closing of my show." He describes it as casual and open. "It's pretty free-flowing. I wanted it to be an environment where multiple people could be involved in the cooking process. People like to gather around and exchange stories—and everyone wants to get involved in cutting something or flipping something, or even just opening a beer." And though he currently has a built-in gas grill with an infrared rotisserie function, he's had various grills over the years, so he speaks from experience, offering the following advice: "Size doesn't always matter. You cook for smaller groups more than you cook for big ones, and if the grill is too big it takes too long to heat up. If it's large, check how many chambers there are." He says that heat recovery—how long the grill takes to heat up and then recover its heat after you've opened it to put the food on—is one important consideration, as is a good grease-management system.

In terms of kitchen layout, he says, "You want to have proximity to the house for movement of food and people. It might be only ten steps from the house, but if you multiply that by the number of times you have to bring things out from the kitchen, it's a lot." And, he advises homeowners to outfit their outdoor cooking space as fully as possible. "If you have three bedrooms and add a fourth you don't move the furniture from one of the other bedrooms every time someone comes to sleep in the new one. Set up the outdoor kitchen like a real kitchen, with condiments, cutting boards, knives, and so on, so you're not running inside all the time."

Finally, he says, get help if you need it. "Bring in professionals early in the process. From a mechanical standpoint, some things might not be possible—due to the layout of a pool or a garden bed or a retaining wall, for example. You'll need to check codes and plans so you're not digging through power lines or an in-ground sprinkler."

DISHING DIRT

Only the most fully outfitted outdoor kitchens typically include dishwashers, and even then only the ones that are built under some sort of shelter. However, if you plan to do most of your cooking outdoors for a large part of the year, it can make sense to include all the same appliances outdoors as you would inside. Choose a dishwasher with a stainless steel exterior panel as well as a stainless steel tub. Look for a model designed to accommodate oversized commercial-style cookware; a dishwasher's not much help if it can't clean the pan in which you marinated your ribs or your favorite stockpot. If you can't incorporate a dishwasher, try to plan some sort of undercounter storage, either a low shelf or a cabinet, so you can stow dirty dishes out of sight until the meal is over and you can shuttle them to the dishwasher inside.

Garbage disposal is another practical consideration, and, again, one that's more complicated than it initially may seem. A slide-out trashcan that is concealed within cabinetry when not in use is a great addition to the outdoor

A sink with running water is a great convenience in an outdoor kitchen, but running plumbing lines from the house can be expensive and difficult, particularly if you live in a cold climate. Many homeowners opt instead to hook a garden hose to an outdoor sink and then simply disconnect the hose in winter.

kitchen. But—and it's a big but—unlike indoors where rolling the unit closed is the end of it, outdoors you'll need to be vigilant about removing the trash each night to a sealed garbage can. Otherwise, you'll be inviting the neighborhood animal population for an after-hours feast, and chances are you'd prefer the local raccoons and bears eat their dinner in the woods.

KEEPING YOUR COOL

Unless your outdoor kitchen is a long walk from the house, you don't really need to include a refrigerator in your plans, but it certainly is a handy helper if you can. Imagine this: Instead of lugging trays of meat and vegetables outside to the grill, you just reach into your undercounter refrigerator and pull out the steaks you've left there to marinate and the vegetables you picked in the garden that morning. You finalize the prep work, pop them on the grill, and you're all set. Or, instead of filling a cooler full of ice and corralling your husband to help you haul it out to the patio to fill with bottles of beer and soda for your guests, you simply serve them from your outdoor beverage center, filling their glasses with ice from the outdoor ice maker.

It's easy to see why many homeowners opt to include a refrigerator in their outdoor kitchen, and it's equally easy to find a manufacturer that produces one. Most have stainless steel exteriors and tempered-glass interior shelves. You'll find models built just for chilling wine and others for dispensing beer. Sizes vary, as do interior configurations and price. If you do decide to purchase an outdoor refrigerator, make sure you use it to its fullest potential. Keep it stocked with all the condiments you use regularly outside: ketchup, mustard, hot sauce, steak sauce, barbecue sauce, pickles, salad dressing, mayonnaise, sour cream, salsa, and so on. Similarly, keep a bar refrigerator filled with the basics: fruit juices, seltzer and sparkling water, soda, beer, and white wine.

A sink with running water makes preparation and cleanup much easier. Before installing a water line, you will need to consider plumbing, along with winter weather and drainage concerns.

A few of the different refrigeration options follow:

UNDERCOUNTER REFRIGERATOR

Undercounter refrigerators, designed to be built into cabinetry, come in a range of sizes, most commonly 24" (61 cm) and 15" (38 cm) wide. Exteriors are usually stainless steel; interior shelves are tempered glass. Look for a model with variable temperature control.

FULL-SIZE REFRIGERATOR

If your outdoor kitchen is large, fully protected from the elements, and located in a warm climate, you might opt to install a regular interior-style refrigerator. Just check with the manufacturer to ensure that it will operate properly in your climate and that installation in an open-air setting won't void the warranty.

REFRIGERATOR DRAWERS

Another popular indoor option also can be a good choice for well-protected outdoor kitchens: Refrigerator drawers can be installed in numerous different configurations. Place one next to the prep sink, for instance, so you can clean vegetables easily, and another by the grill, so you can transfer meat to the cooking surface with a minimum of steps. Another might go on the outside of the grill island, so kids and guests can help themselves to drinks and snacks without passing through the prep zone.

BEVERAGE DISPENSER

Essentially a tap surrounded by a stainless steel cabinet—often on wheels—this accessory is ideal for the bar crowd.

WINE REFRIGERATOR

This type of refrigerator has two or more cooling zones (unlike a regular refrigerator, which has one), allowing you to store different types of wine at the ideal temperature. Interior shelves are often slanted forward, so the corks are kept wet.

Including a refrigerator in your plans will make preparing an entire meal in your outdoor kitchen much easier and more efficient, and will cut down on trips back and forth between the house and the grill area.

ICE MAKER

A must-have for anyone who entertains frequently, an ice maker does what it says: It makes ice. Look for a model that makes a large amount—say 35 pounds (16 kg)—in a short time.

A DIFFERENT VIEW

Though it can be tempting to pack your outdoor kitchen with every appliance you can find, what you'll end up with if you do this is a kitchen that just happens to be outdoors. Remember what drew you to cooking outdoors in the first place. Maybe it was a camping experience—smelling a wood fire, making do with what you had, and enjoying every bite the more for it. Or maybe it was the laid-back attitude of a weekend cookout—a far cry from the monotony of the perfectly choreographed weeknight dinner prepared inside. If you over-appliance your outdoor kitchen, if you get too fancy, you might lose some of the appeal of outdoor cooking in the process. There's nothing wrong with buying the latest grill or smoker, of course, but don't feel that you have to include every little luxury. There's something to be said for roughing it a little (even if your outdoor kitchen is worth as much as a small car).

And, because so much outdoor cooking revolves around entertaining, it's nice to give your guests something to do. Skip the motorized rotisserie and let your brothers-in-law take turns tending the chickens. Forget the dishwasher and let your neighbor rinse the plates. Leave the ice maker at the showroom and pick a clever vessel—a wheelbarrow, say, or an old-fashioned washbasin—to hold the bags of ice you bought at the grocery store—you'll have an instant conversation starter. The bottom line: Take stock of what you really want and need before you start shopping; otherwise, it's very easy to be seduced by shining stainless steel.

STORE MORE

Without the right storage, your well-planned outdoor kitchen will be cluttered and clumsy, unattractive to look at, and uncomfortable to work in. And although an outdoor kitchen may not have—or need—nearly as much storage as an indoor kitchen, the guiding principles are the same. First, before you order cabinets (or plan custom units) make an item-by-item list of everything you plan to store in them, from utensils and tools to plates and dishes, pots and pans, napkins, potholders, and toothpicks—you name it. Second, designate storage for everything on your list: a mix of cabinets, drawers, shelves, closets, and even racks and hooks. Third, plan for a little extra—you can never have too much

When shopping for an outdoor refrigerator, look for one with an interior designed to hold odd-shaped items, such as trays of hors d'oeuvres.

storage space. If you've done your job, you'll find yourself working more efficiently and saving steps. Everything you need will be right at hand when you need it. Because storage is such an essential element to a successful work-space, it can make good sense to consult with a designer during this phase of the project. If you're not working with an architect or kitchen designer, many home centers have on-staff designers who can help you maximize the storage potential of your space.

Storage in the outdoor kitchen comes in a wide range of forms. The most basic outdoor kitchen might have a cabinet underneath a freestanding grill (though a propane tank might take up most of this space in liquid propane models). Deluxe kitchens could have as many cabinets and drawers as their indoor counterparts. Most outdoor kitchens will fall someplace in the middle.

Storage will keep your kitchen efficient and uncluttered; you can really never have enough. In addition to undercounter cabinets, a full-height closet like this one is a great addition to your plans. Use it to stow less-often-used items like lanterns, party candles, and linens.

GRILL ISLAND

One of the most popular options for storage is to build or buy a grill island—basically a countertop into which a built-in gas grill is set. Depending on the size, the grill island has counterspace on one or both sides of the grill and cabinet space underneath. This space is a good place to keep tools, rolls of paper towels, a fire extinguisher, and other basic essentials.

THE MORE THE MERRIER

If your setup will be more extensive, it can make sense to include significantly more storage. For example, you may want several drawers for the utensils you use outdoors, as well as knives and other cooking tools. Cabinets for dishes and glasses are another nice convenience, though you may need to move breakables indoors when temperatures turn cold enough to crack glassware. And don't forget the specialized storage that few kitchens have but most need: shallow drawers for table linens, tall slots for trays, and deep drawers for heavy pots and roasting pans. You may also want to devote a cabinet or two to frequently used dry goods like spices, rice, pasta, flour, sugar, and the like. An undersink cabinet is the perfect place to keep cleaning supplies. And for larger items that are used frequently but not every day—such as table lanterns, tiki torches, and candles—it's great to have a nearby closet available for party supplies. Cabinet materials really run the gamut. Basically, anything that can withstand the elements is fine; stainless steel is always a safe bet as it is largely impervious to water and sun and also critter resistant. Choose a style that suits your personal style and enhances the look of your outdoor kitchen. Accessorize with hardware that feels good to the touch and operates smoothly and easily.

CRITTER CONTROL

It's just about the last thing you want to think about when planning your outdoor kitchen, but because it's going to be outside, you have to consider how to keep wildlife at bay. The most obvious solution is not to store foodstuffs outside. But, because that may cut down on the efficiency of your design, you can take some precautionary measures, such as storing all food products (rice, beans, and so on) in airtight tin or stainless steel bins inside tightly closing stainless steel cabinets. Garbage should be removed from the outdoor kitchen immediately after each meal and put in a closed, locking container. In areas where bears are a problem, consult your local animal control authorities for appropriate precautions concerning disposal of trash.

Stainless steel is the material of choice for outdoor cabinetry. It holds up well to the elements and protects its contents against the curious explorations of unwanted animal visitors.

Storage doesn't have to be built in. If you have a freestanding grill (or even if you don't), a portable standalone cart like this one can be a handy addition to your cooking area.

SURFACE REPORT

To work efficiently in your kitchen, you'll need ample counter-space. The side tables on a freestanding grill really aren't enough. They're a handy landing spot for a plate of grilled vegetables or an empty marinade container, but there's not enough space to let you slice and dice on them, nor can you plate up dinner for four. For all but the most basic prep and cleanup functions, you'll need a proper countertop. Ideally, your outdoor kitchen should have three counterspaces—one on each side of the grill (where you'll leave the containers that held the meat before it was cooked, and the platter to which you'll transfer the food when it's done) and another nearby. This one should be a large, open surface where you can clean vegetables, assemble hors d'oeuvres, and serve a buffet, if you like.

Your options are not as wide ranging as they would be indoors, but you'll still find plenty of surfacing types from which to choose. The most common options follow:

CERAMIC TILE

Affordable ceramic tile has much to recommend it, not least of which is the limitless array of colors, sizes, and styles available. As long as it's exterior grade, tile is fine for outdoor applications, which is why it's a favorite material for outdoor kitchens. Things to watch out for include grout, which must be sealed with a penetrating water-based sealant and still may stain, and heavy pots and pans that can crack ceramic tile if dropped.

NATURAL STONE

Nonporous, heat-resistant, and beautiful, granite is one of the most attractive options for an outdoor kitchen counter-top—and also one of the most expensive. Still, if you're a stickler for performance and return on investment, granite is a good choice for you. Another option is soapstone. Long a choice for laboratory countertops, soapstone has an appealing low-luster finish and is soft to the touch—and it's less expensive than granite (though it's also not as resilient

The paving you choose for your outdoor kitchen and living areas is just as important as countertop surfacing and should integrate well with the architecture of your house. Note here how the variegated pattern of the tile complements the rustic style of the natural stone siding and columns.

and may scratch and wear in places over tim[e] can camouflage scratches with an applicati[on] sandpaper and a coat of mineral oil, soapst[one] way to go if you insist on absolutely pristi[ne]

STAINLESS STEEL

Hygienic and ideal for outdoor applications, stainless steel countertops also have a chic, high-tech look many outdoor cooks love. However, stainless countertops must be custom fabricated, which can be expensive. You can also purchase high-grade restaurant-quality stainless steel work tables at restaurant supply stores inexpensively and in several lengths (they start at $200 for a 6'–8' [1.8–2.4 m] table), or a rolling stainless steel trolley.

CONCRETE

Not just for patios anymore, concrete countertops are beautiful and durable, whether used indoors or out. They can be poured in place or fabricated off site and colored with pigments to match any color in the rainbow.

WOOD

Though it's a great choice for indoor countertops, butcher block should not be used as an outdoor countertop because it tends to warp, split, and buckle when exposed to moisture and sunlight.

LAMINATE

Affordable and available in a nearly limitless range of colors and patterns, laminate surfacing can fade in sunlight, so its use should be limited to covered areas. Laminate can also scratch, chip, and burn, so treat it as carefully as you would in an indoor kitchen.

QUARTZ SURFACES

It may look like granite but this man-made stone surfacing isn't up to all-weather outdoor use—yet (technological developments in this area are promising). Keep this beautiful material for sheltered areas.

Stone is a natural choice for an outdoor space where countertops must stand up to more than the usual amount of kitchen abuse, including rain, wind, snow, and intense heat. Granite, which is impervious to stains and will not burn if you place a hot pot directly on its surface, is one good option; soap-stone, slate, or tumbled marble are alternatives.

For a kitchen that's as easy to maintain as it is attractive, choose paving that you can hose off at the end of each meal. A subtle texture will keep the surface safe and nonslip.

SOLID SURFACES

Solid surfacing, a solid acrylic material available in a dizzying array of patterns and colors, is another option. Beloved by indoor cooks for its renewable surface—scratches and stains can be sanded out—and potential for personalization—edges can be profiled, the surface can be inlaid with decorative motifs—solid surfacing can fade when exposed to sunlight, so use only under cover outdoors. Solid surfacing is not heat resistant; to prevent scorch marks, always set hot pots and dishes on a trivet.

TOP SELECTIONS

Deciding which type of countertop surfacing to use depends on a number of factors: the layout and location of your kitchen, your cooking habits, your budget, and, not least of all, your personal style. Location is probably the most defining detail when it comes to choosing a surfacing material. If your outdoor kitchen is exposed to sunlight, you should stay away from laminate, solid surfacing, or quartz surfacing, which may fade over time. But, if your kitchen will be covered, you can use these materials with impunity. A seaside site is another limiting factor: salt water and moisture can damage any material, but stainless steel holds up better than most.

Next, consider the way you cook. If you like the convenience of setting a hot pan right on the counter, then ceramic tile or granite is a good choice for you. You can't cut directly on any of these materials without dulling a knife blade, so you should plan to store a couple of large cutting boards nearby (plastic will weather best). Want easy cleanup? Stay away from ceramic tile—even sealed grout has a way of attracting dirt over time (although a time-consuming task, the grout can be dug out and redone). Stainless countertops can be hosed off, literally.

If budget is a concern, on the other hand, ceramic tile is a good choice. Solid color-field tiles are quite inexpensive, and you can personalize the look with a few judiciously placed pricey decorator tiles. Finally, ask yourself how your surfacing choice will impact the overall look of the space. For a rustic look, go with a natural stone with honed or rough edges; for a sleek, modern effect, opt for tinted concrete or stainless steel.

DESIGN IDEAS

Your countertops dominate a large portion of the visual space of your outdoor kitchen, so it's smart to make them pull their weight stylewise. Don't settle for the basic slab of granite or a simple tiled surface. Make the space uniquely yours by specifying personal details such as rough edges on stone counters or edges with a delicate ogee profile. For tiled counters, choose the tiles yourself and design a pattern for their installation. Under covered areas, solid-surfacing counters can be inlaid with contrasting colors in a design of your choosing, and edges can be profiled or given a striped effect.

COMPARING COSTS

Countertop materials range widely in price. Here's a general idea of price ranges for some of the most popular options.

INEXPENSIVE	MID-RANGE	MOST COSTLY
Ceramic tile	Butcher block	Solid surfacing
Laminate	Stainless steel	Quartz surfacing
	Soapstone	Granite
	Concrete	

There's a certain romance about cooking over an open flame—the flicker of the fire, the smell of the smoke—but this romance can heat up all too quickly. Hot spots on the grill can flare up, causing foods to ignite almost before you've noticed the problem. Outdoor cooking appliances get very, very hot, and it can be easy to burn yourself if you're not careful. Paving can become slippery when wet; even countertop corners can cause bumps and bruises. It's easy to plan a safe cooking space, if you take the following precautions:

- Always adhere to local codes. They're there for a reason—to protect you and your property.

- Make sure all grills, electrical outlets, and lights are installed properly, by a professional, and that all working parts are in order. Use only the type of fuel specified for the grill unit.

- Consider installing a vent hood above the grill.

- Construct grill islands and adjacent cabinetry from noncombustible materials. Keep cooking appliances away from combustible overhangs and siding material.

- Choose textured, nonslip paving. Mark all steps with a contrasting band of tape and install handrails where possible.

- Round the corners of countertops.

- Keep a fire extinguisher handy at all times.

- Keep children out of the cooking area.

Think carefully about color, as well. Choose a color and pattern that will reinforce the theme of the kitchen, the exterior of your house, and the landscape; for example, a soft sand-and-gold granite for a beachfront kitchen, or a sleek black soapstone for a contemporary workspace. Materials with large particulates in their design hide dirt better than solid-colored surfaces do.

WHAT'S UNDERFOOT?

If you'll be building an outdoor kitchen from scratch—as opposed to adding one to an existing patio or deck—you'll need to decide what materials to use on the "floor." Because the paving material will probably extend out of the kitchen area into adjacent dining and lounging spaces, it's important to choose something as pretty as it is practical. Your first priority, though, is to choose a material that will create an even, level surface. This rules out options such as gravel or fieldstone pavers, which have a naturally uneven surface.

Instead, opt for brick or man-made paving stones, flat slate, or concrete. Concrete can be stained, stamped, and inlaid to give it a colored or textured look. For a personal touch, arrange brick or pavers in a herringbone or other pattern, or mix more than one material—brick and concrete, for instance. Or, use different materials to designate different areas of use: light, cool concrete around the pool, with a step up to a slate patio that flows into the outdoor kitchen.

Outdoor-grade tile is another good option for the kitchen; just make sure you choose one with a slight texture, to prevent them from becoming slippery when wet. Using the same tile on both the floor and the countertops—larger tiles on the floor, of course—can lend visual unity to the kitchen area and set it apart from other outdoor areas paved in a contrasting material.

CHAPTER THREE
ENTERTAINING ALFRESCO
BRINGING THE ELEGANCE OUT-OF-DOORS

If you're like most people, your motivation for building an outdoor kitchen is not to give yourself another place to whip up Wednesday-night dinner for the kids. More likely, it's to make outdoor entertaining easier and more enjoyable because, as you've probably noticed, guests like to be where the action is. Inside, they forsake the comfortable, elegant living room to crowd around the kitchen island to watch you chop parsley. Outside, it's the same thing: Everyone wants to be near the grill—some to help cook, others to offer "helpful" comments, others to watch while sipping a cold beer. There's just something about the creative process of cooking that attracts guests like moths to the flame—so planning a proper outdoor kitchen not only offers the cook convenience and efficiency, it gives your family and friends a comfortable place to gather during a party.

As you plan, think about how the space will work for a group. For example, even the smallest grill island will have a chunk of counterspace at one end; this is the perfect place for a friend to perch while you cook or to help with some of the prep work. More extensive outdoor kitchens can include even more guest-friendly features. A bar with stools and cocktail fixings is a festive addition, and one that will double as a lunch station for the kids by day. Outdoor kitchens go hand-in-hand with outdoor dining areas, of course, and you'll want to plan a dining space for at least six and outfit it with style and sophistication. Lounging areas with sofas or soft armchairs are another nice touch. You'll be able to serve cocktails and dessert in a relaxed setting, just as you would indoors.

A well-planned entertaining area places the comfort of its occupants at center stage. This lovely space combines cooking, dining, and lounging areas characterized by comfy furnishings, a sheltered enclosure, and soft mood lighting.

THE BAR CROWD

If you've ever spent any time at a tropical resort, you probably remember whiling away the evening perched on a bar stool sipping a daiquiri, or escaping the sun at lunchtime to nibble conch fritters at the beachside snack bar. There's just something undeniably relaxing about drinking or eating at a bar: The very act feels like an escape. But unless you spend a large chunk of your time at a place like Basil's Bar in Mustique, just about the only way to capture that fun, festive feeling on a regular basis is by including a bar in your own outdoor kitchen.

Practically speaking, bars provide a lot of benefits in an outdoor cooking and entertaining space. For one thing, a bar gives guests a natural gathering point, a place where they can stand with drink or snack in hand and chat, without feeling awkward or out of place. Because the bar is usually attached to the kitchen area itself or built nearby, friends can also watch the cook—from a slight distance, though, so neither they nor you feel imposed on. For another, a bar keeps your workspace clean by providing a dedicated area for cocktail fixings, glasses, and trays of hors d'oeuvres. It's much easier to cook if you're not working around a bunch of lemon slices and used napkins.

You can also think of the bar as an extra dining table. It's the perfect place for breakfast or a casual lunch, and during big parties some people can sit at the bar for dinner (kids, perhaps). And, because bars are by their very nature somewhat exotic, they give you a great creative outlet. If your outdoor kitchen is covered, you can string the roof with hundreds of tiny lights, outfit it like a grass hut, or choose stools just like the ones in *Casablanca* or your favorite surf shack.

DESIGN DETAILS

Because you want your bar to be a fully functioning part of the outdoor kitchen, it's important to make it an integrated part of the overall design—not an afterthought. First, think about where you want the bar. Should it be freestanding, a few feet from the kitchen, or attached to one end of the kitchen island? If it's attached to the kitchen counter, its

If you don't want to build a bar—or if you live in a cold climate where it's important to be able to move kitchen elements inside in the winter—a freestanding bar can make sense. These units are available in a wide range of sizes and materials from home centers and barbecue retailers.

SMALL WONDERS

Because your outdoor kitchen should approximate the efficiency of your indoor workspace, it makes sense to include as many indoor amenities as you can. Small appliances—those handy helpers that make cooking so much faster and easier—are as indispensable outdoors as they are indoors. Make a list of the appliances you can't live without. A blender probably tops your list, followed, perhaps, by a mini food processor. Shop for heavy-duty models, and plan to store them in a covered area, ideally, inside a cabinet. And don't forget to factor electrical outlets into your kitchen plans. The counter should have several outlets, and the bar should have at least one. Note that even table umbrellas come with built-in outlets these days; ask your outdoor furniture showroom about them.

height will hide the detritus of food prep and cleanup from sight of the dining area, so you might opt to place it in front of the dining table. Doing so gives you the added advantage of a pass-through sidebar or buffet station. Choose surfacing that coordinates with the outdoor kitchen—and that's easy to clean—but that puts its best foot forward. After all, the bar is a focal point for guests.

Still, you can include features that make it useful as well as pretty. A bar sink is a natural addition. This feature makes mixing drinks much easier, but it also lets the bar double as a prep and cleanup zone during large parties. An undercounter refrigerator and ice maker are also smart additions. Your guests can help themselves, and children can get drinks without coming into the hot cooking area.

If you like the idea of including a bar in your outdoor kitchen but don't have the budget to build one, take heart: Many manufacturers offer freestanding, portable bar carts or stands with a wide range of features from compartments for necessities like lemon and lime wedges and ice, and even storage for glasses. Look online at the websites of grill manufacturers (see Resources, page 156), and you'll find numerous styles from which to choose.

DINING OUT

What comes first—the outdoor kitchen or the outdoor dining table? For most of us, it's probably the latter: until recently, few homeowners have had much in the way of an outdoor kitchen—a grill doesn't count—but most people have some sort of outdoor eating area, even if it's just a picnic table. So there's really no way—and no reason—to design an effective outdoor kitchen without planning a comfortable, attractive dining area to go with it. The dining table creates a focal point for the entire outdoor living space—a destination during parties and a useful surface the rest of the time. You may even find that you use the dining area more than the kitchen itself: to catch up with some work on a Sunday afternoon; to eat cereal you've carried out from the indoor kitchen; or to sip lemonade with friends after a dip in the pool.

But designing a successful outdoor dining "room" is much more than sticking a table and chairs somewhere near the outdoor kitchen. Instead, you need to look at it as a separate space, with its own identity to match its range of uses, and then outfit it accordingly with furnishings, lighting, and accessories chosen for their style and use. If you do, the dining area will create a charming setting for your parties large and small, a backdrop for whimsical table settings, a canvas for your beautifully prepared food, and a welcoming center for your guests.

THE RIGHT STYLE

The look of your dining area will in large part determine the overall style of your outdoor living spaces, so it's important to choose a dining set carefully. Whatever your personal preference, you'll find an option on the market to match it. For a traditional look, you might choose a teak table with gate-back chairs. A tile-topped table with an iron base and fancy scrolled iron chairs would create a more exotic atmosphere. For a down-home country character, you can't go wrong with the classic redwood picnic table; you can use accessories and table settings to add a little sophistication. As you shop, look for additional items, like an umbrella—a must-have to protect you and your guests from the hot sun—or a lazy Susan, which is a fun icebreaker for a dinner party.

THE PERFECT SETTING

When it comes to hosting the perfect party, there's no avoiding the fact that your table setting is one of the strongest indications of your personal style and your attention to detail. It's also one of the best opportunities

to exercise your sense of fun and to inject an element of whimsy into your outdoor living space. How to plan a table that shouts "wow!" (even quietly)? Just pick a starting point—it might be your menu or the date of the party—then dress the table accordingly. For example, if you're serving a Thai sampler with chicken satay and jasmine rice, you might give the table a spicy Asian look, with hot-colored linens (bright pink or rich orange, perhaps), bamboo trays, chopsticks, and colorful paper lanterns hanging in the trees. Fresh flowers—floating in a shallow bowl of water, perhaps—complete the picture. An autumn barbecue, on the other hand, would get a totally different treatment: warm reds,

Outdoor dining is one of the greatest joys of warm weather seasons. This stone and wood arrangement takes the traditional picnic table to a new level of style and sophistication.

PAULA DEEN

Sometimes, it takes a difficult situation to create a success story. Take, for example, beloved Food TV chef Paula Deen. Though today she's known the world over for her warm wit, charming accent, and scrumptious food, it wasn't so long ago that she was the newly divorced mom of two starting out on her own. This steel magnolia looked to her Southern-fried roots for inspiration and turned to her kitchen for salvation. And, in 1989, her first business, a home-based lunch delivery service called The Bag Lady, was born. Two years later, Savannah's lunch crowd had created such a demand for Deen's sandwiches that the business had outgrown its quarters; she and her sons opened their first restaurant, The Lady and Sons, in Savannah's south side. Five years after that they moved to their city market location, a downtown setting for one of Savannah's most popular restaurants. Four best-selling cookbooks, one Oprah appearance, and one hit Food Network television show later, Deen is still cooking at home, in style, and with a strong Southern accent.

Professional Help

Paula Deen has just finished building a new home on Wilmington Island in Savannah, Georgia, and as you might expect from a true daughter of the South, the outdoor kitchen—and the rest of the house—is designed for hospitality. But first let's get one thing straight. "It's (my new husband) *Michael's* outdoor kitchen," she laughs. "He's the proud owner of about six grills, which he just loves!" It quickly becomes clear, however, that Deen had just as big a hand in the kitchen's design as her husband. "We just built this wonderful space," she says. "Twenty-five people can gather there easily. It's right on the water, on Turner's Creek, and we can sit there on our rockers and watch the dolphins swim by." In addition to the great location, the kitchen is outfitted to the teeth with the latest conveniences. "We have an ice maker out there, and a sink with a commercial dishwashing attachment, so you don't have to worry about fitting a large pot under the spout. And naturally we're installing a TV out there," says Deen.

Ambience is in equally generous supply. "We have fans, and old-timey hanging lights on cords, and beautiful countertops of concrete flecked with oyster shells. We're doing some landscaping with an herb garden right there with a fountain in the middle that our dogs can drink out of." But Deen didn't go all out on the outdoor kitchen just for herself and her husband; they like to entertain their family outdoors as well and needed to accommodate a crowd. "We've got about twenty or twenty-two family members," she explains, "and I wanted to make sure there was plenty of room for everyone to sit. So we have bar stools around that beautiful countertop."

Layout was another important consideration. "It started out as an L-shape space, but then we did away with the L—I thought people might get pinned in." When the gang's all there, Michael uses a big electric grill that will "hold a bunch of chicken for when the family is all over. It has a container that you can add wood to (for a smoky flavor)," but at other times they use their ceramic Kamado-style cooker. "It's fabulous—it cooks so hot and so fast," she says. Deen's advice for homeowners designing their own outdoor kitchen? "Figure out what you want your kitchen to do for you," she says, "and plan it around that."

Don't forget to dress the hors d'oeuvres table. Fresh flowers are the easiest way to pretty-up a table. Arranging foods on simple plates and trays keeps the emphasis on what you're serving.

golds, and russets; corn stalks and pumpkins; comfort food with apple cider amidst the falling leaves would do the trick nicely.

If you're setting the table for a special occasion, feel free to make an even bigger statement. Branch out beyond pretty linens and dishes to unique place cards and theme-related table decorations. For instance, you might handwrite each guest's name on a large, flat leaf and tuck it into a rustic napkin ring at each place. Or, for a beachfront gathering, you might strew the center of the table with sand, shells, and bits of beach glass; tiny sailboats could bear place cards for each spot.

PARTY TIME

You may also want to set a table for a buffet. Stack the plates at one end, but keep bundles of napkins and silverware at the other, so guests can pile their plates high without struggling to keep a handle on their flatware at the same time. Label each dish so guests will know what they're eating, and make sure you provide a range of options—with at least one vegetarian choice.

Music is a particularly important ingredient when it comes to setting the mood for a big party. For a sophisticated atmosphere, go with Cole Porter or George and Ira Gershwin; an all-American theme might merit a little

FOCUS ON: COMFORT

If you live in a warm climate—or anyplace summer days get hot and steamy—you know that it's no fun to be outdoors when temperatures soar. To make the investment in your outdoor kitchen a wise one, take care to make your outdoor living spaces comfortable and usable for as long a season as possible. A few good ideas follow:

Shade. Providing shade for your kitchen, dining area, and lounging areas is goal number one. You might simply place the kitchen under the overhang of your home's roof or in a spot where trees provide shelter. A pergola planted with vines or a solid roof overhead are other good options. To lend shade during the hottest times of day and light the rest of the time, you might opt for a motorized retractable awning.

Fans. Outdoor fans, suspended from the roof of a porch or semienclosed outdoor kitchen, keep the air moving in your outdoor living space, making it more comfortable on hot day. Look for a fan that's UL rated for "wet locations," as opposed to "damp locations"; the former have seals and grommets to prevent moisture from penetrating the motor and electrical elements, plastic weather-resistant blades, and stainless steel hardware.

Misting Systems. Misters force water through a nozzle to produce superfine droplets of water that cool thanks to "flash evaporation" when they reach the hot air—without wetting the surrounding area. These systems work best in hot, dry areas—in humid locales, they just add humidity to the air. In the right setting, they can lower the air temperature by as much as 25°F (4°C) degrees. (For more on misting systems, see Resources, page 156.)

---

country picking; a more formal occasion would be well suited by some quiet chamber music.

If you're hosting a particularly large group, you may need to rent extra tables and chairs, plates, glasses, silverware, and linens, and even a tent—or two. All these and more are available from local party rental firms; check your telephone directory business pages for listings. While you're at it, consider hiring a caterer and some musicians: you'll be able to relax and enjoy the party instead of standing over a grill tending the food, and live music always gets a party started.

LOUNGE ACT

When you're not cooking or eating outdoors, what are you doing? Just hanging out, probably. So while you're planning an outdoor kitchen, it's a good time to plan comfortable, inviting socializing areas as well. Lounging areas—the outdoor living room, you might say—can take almost any form you like, from a simple setup of a bench and a couple of

You don't need a lot of room to create a comfortable spot for your family and friends to sit and relax. A rustic table and a pair of benches placed in the garden will do the trick nicely.

chairs to a line of reclining chaise lounges to a full-blown arrangement of upholstered sofas, armchairs, and love seats. Or, you might want a combination of all these types of seating.

Because the main function of an outdoor lounging area is to make yourself and your guests comfortable, comfort should be your focus as you plan and shop. In terms of location, pick a spot that's sheltered—if not by an actual overhead covering, at least by some trees or other plantings. You want to create an atmosphere of intimacy. Also consider wind patterns. You won't want to lounge very long if you're getting a faceful of smoke from the grill. Then think about how many people will use the space, and how. If you want a spot to sit after dinner or a place for your teenagers to hang around by the pool, your needs will be different than if you'll be hosting large groups, either formally or informally. Don't forget the details: side tables for drinks and bowls of chips, a coffee table for trays of appetizers, a heater for cold evenings, lighting, and decorative elements.

LINKING INSIDE AND OUT

An outdoor living space doesn't exist in a vacuum. It's inextricably linked to the architecture of your house and to your interior living spaces. Therefore, it's a good idea to

consider the style of your indoor lounging areas when you plan the ones outside. Physically connecting indoor and outdoor living rooms is one possibility. Sliding glass or French doors at one end of the living room or family room can open onto a patio. This setup is a great way to provide some flexibility—open both doors so that people can circulate in and out freely, or close them to keep the indoors and outdoors separate. But even if you don't choose to—or cannot—connect your interior and exterior lounging areas, you can still create a visual and emotional link between them. Keeping in mind that outdoor rooms are naturally more casual than those indoors, you might choose furniture in shapes that echo the pieces inside. For example, if your living room is formal with traditional-style furniture and rich fabrics, you might select wicker outdoor furniture, soft upholstery, and throw pillows in delicate patterns. A more contemporary look inside might find its outdoor counterpart in sleek aluminum and glass furniture with angular lines and tailored cushions. Be creative, but remember that your outdoor living area is as much a part of your home as your dining room—and it deserves just as much attention.

HOW MUCH IS ENOUGH?

For a simple outdoor kitchen with a small dining area, you'll probably find that two to four wicker chairs with soft cushions offer plenty of lounging space. Add a small coffee table between the chairs, and you have an intimate conversation center. Expand the scene a bit, and you might want to add a wicker sofa with end tables and outdoor lamps or lanterns suspended from the ceiling or overhead covering (even from a branch). An even larger plan might call for a second seating area. This time, alter the look a little: a teak bench and side chairs, or a poolside combination of lounge chairs. Basically, the amount of seating you incorporate should be determined by the way you plan to use the space.

EXTRA, EXTRA

So you've chosen chairs and a sofa or love seat, side tables, and a coffee table. Are you ready to entertain your closest cronies in your new outdoor living room? Sure—unless you want to make it really special. If you want to create a hangout spot that's as stylish as you are, you'll want more.

Another way to save space without sacrificing comfort is to combine dining and lounging areas. If dining area seating is soft and inviting, you won't need a separate relaxation zone.

Fortunately, a number of extras are available that will help make your relaxation zone one your friends will remember for a long time.

First and foremost: outdoor fireplaces are available in a wide range of styles and sizes, in wood-burning and gas models. An outdoor fireplace is a great focal point for any seating area. You can opt for a built-in model—if it's wood-burning you might even want to incorporate an oven for baking pizza and bread—or a freestanding design, firepit, or Mexican chiminea.

Another nice touch is an umbrella, either freestanding or as part of a dining table. Market umbrellas come in a wide range of sizes and colors; some even include built-in outlets (handy for plugging in a blender to make tableside margaritas).

Built-in speakers—or speakers mounted to the outside of your house—make it a snap to pipe your favorite tunes outdoors during parties.

Mood lighting, of course, is a necessity for any occasion. In addition to integrated lighting, consider stringing strands of lanterns or holiday lights from awnings, umbrellas, pergolas, and roof overhangs. The effect is magical and romantic.

THAT'S ENTERTAINING

An outdoor setting is by far the easiest for any party—as long as the weather cooperates. To ensure that your alfresco fiesta doesn't get soaked, windswept or fried, plan ahead to provide comfort for your guests. If you'll be entertaining frequently and in large numbers, work at least one sheltered area into your design. It might be the kitchen itself, or a covered seating area, a gazebo, or an arbor hung with fragrant floral vines. If the climate where you live is particularly hot, you may wish to incorporate cooling elements like fans or a mister (see Focus On: Comfort on page 79). Design windblocks into the landscaping—the effect will be sheltering and comforting, as well as practical. And a fireplace, in addition to improving the ambience, can keep you toasty on cool evenings, as can a propane-fueled heater (see Resources, page 156).

A true outdoor living room includes all the elements you'd find indoors: a strong decorative theme—here the look is exotic—beautiful fabrics and furnishings, romantic lighting, and a focal point, in this case the central firepit.

HOT TIPS

Designer Chris Barrett of Chris Barrett Design in Santa Monica, California, regularly extends her interior designs to her clients' outdoor rooms, including outdoor kitchens. Her style secrets:

- **Be bold.** "People shouldn't be afraid to take a chance or two. Yes, you want something that can stand up to the elements, but truly think of it as a room—don't just make it functional."

- **Mix old and new.** "If you can, add a little history to any room—you could get an old garden table from the '20s, say. It kind of grounds the space."

- **Consider aesthetics.** "You can use some non-outdoor fabric to soften things up a little bit. And don't be afraid of color."

- **Don't forget lighting.** "It's really important that you can see when you're cooking. In one space I worked on we hung a giant antique lantern from a tree, but we also cheated and put a spotlight above it. It looks as if the lantern is lighting the work area, but it's really the spotlight."

- **Be flexible.** "You can set up an outdoor room anywhere—you don't need a hard (paved) space to do it. Just get a grill on wheels and some pillows. Keep it loose and fun."

If you plan to entertain a lot, design accordingly. A multilevel patio, like this one, creates a number of different areas for guests to congregate while still allowing everyone to circulate freely.

Take a cue from the designers of top resorts and hotels: A well-equipped bar is an entertaining must-have. This outdoor kitchen is ready for a crowd, thanks to its spacious design with room for several tables and capacious bar area.

Your comfort as host and chef—if you're doing the cooking—is equally important, of course. If you know you'll be entertaining regularly, including the appropriate elements in the kitchen will make things run much more smoothly. But if your kitchen will fall into the "budget" category, never fear—you can still entertain in comfort and style; it just takes a little more advance planning.

Well before the party, bring all the dishes, glasses, flatware, and linens you'll need outdoors. Set up the buffet or table as early as you can to have it out of the way; do the

same with flower arrangements. Mix up pitchers of drinks and refrigerate them inside until everyone arrives. Or, set up a do-it-yourself bar on a table outside. No ice maker? Fill a galvanized tub with ice (much prettier than a plastic cooler) and stock it with plenty of beer and soda. For the meal, make sure you have all the vegetables cut and meat prepared long before the first guest arrives, so all you'll have to do is cook it once your friends are milling about. Likewise, choose hors d'oeuvres that you can prepare in advance and set out on trays.

HOW MUCH TO SERVE?

Estimating how much food to buy and prepare for a party can stump even the most practiced host. A few guidelines follow:

Meat, poultry, and fish. Plan 5 to 6 oz. (142 to 170 g) per person for a sit-down dinner, or 4 to 6 oz. (113.5 to 170 g) for a buffet.

Pasta. One pound (0.5 kg) of pasta will feed four to six for a sit-down dinner or eight to twelve at a buffet.

Side dishes. One-cup serving of savory side dish per person; ½ (120 ml) cup of a sweet side dish per person.

Vegetables. Plan one handful of salad per person, and about 1 cup (240 ml) of whole vegetables per person.

Dessert. One portion per person, slightly less if serving multiple desserts.

Libations. One-half bottle of wine per person, or 1 cup (240 ml) of a nonalcoholic beverage.

Hors d'oeuvres. Ten to twelve items per person.

A fireplace is a wonderful addition to a dining or lounging area. It adds instant comfort, both in the practical warmth it provides and the inviting atmosphere the flickering hearth creates.

CROWD CONTROL

For an enjoyable party, large or small, it's of utmost importance that you provide enough space for guests to circulate freely without interrupting the cook or cooks. To keep things moving, plan various gathering zones: for example, a bar at the end of the outdoor kitchen island, a dining table (or two) and chairs, an upholstered seating area, a few lounge chairs, and maybe a bench or glider. This way everyone can gravitate toward some destination, and you won't have clumps of people standing around the kitchen while you try to prevent fifteen chicken breasts from turning into charcoal.

It's also a good idea to provide some sort of entertainment, even if it's in the form of activities the guests perform themselves. Dancing is one of the easiest activities to organize—just clear a chunk of patio and play some toe-tapping tunes. Charades or a similar party game is another fun option. During the day, you might organize a game of croquet, or plan a walk in the woods. The point is to give your guests something that will bring them together—so everyone will feel comfortable and relaxed.

CHAPTER FOUR

SETTING THE MOOD
EXPRESSING YOUR INDIVIDUAL STYLE

Personality: In any room, indoors or out, it's what separates the wheat from the chaff, the dazzling from the dull, and what makes a space inviting and warm and special. Just think about the rooms (and outdoor rooms) you've admired in the past. Chances are each one has something a little different about it—its owner's penchant for the color green, a particularly comfy sofa, an alluring lighting scheme—and this is what you want to bring to your own outdoor spaces: a sense of your own individual style, your likes and dislikes, your habits and interests. How to do this in an area where the opportunities to use things like fabrics and carpet, wallcoverings, and wall art are limited at best? Well, you have to be creative, but it's still absolutely possible to create an intimate, personal space with outdoor furniture, hardscaping, and landscaping.

There's no reason to stick a couple of chairs and a glass-topped table on your patio and leave it at that, or to consider the design of your outdoor kitchen finished as soon as you've rolled the grill into position. These spaces may be functional, but they won't encourage you or your guests to linger long. On the other hand, a kitchen with tiles you chose yourself that remind you of a long-ago trip to Italy, furniture that begs people to sit and stay awhile, low tables with flickering candles, and lighting that casts an intriguing glow will make your investment worthwhile. So, just as you would when outfitting any indoor space, approach the look of your outdoor rooms with loving care, attending to every detail, even the smallest.

Creating atmosphere in your outdoor living areas can be easy. The idea is to lend your space a sense of style, no matter how simple the setup. Although this workspace is tucked into an exterior corner of the house, it feels like a true "room," thanks to the arched ironwork trellis and gate at one end.

Answering a few simple questions can help you identify the style that suits you best.

- **Do I like things with a symmetrical design or a more free-form look?** If symmetry is your preference, a traditional approach to outdoor decor is probably best for you; free-form styles work best with rustic or exotic schemes.

- **What kinds of textures appeal to me?** Rough and natural? Sleek and smooth? Something in between? Rustic design is often characterized by rough-hewn textures, whereas more contemporary styles use materials that are shiny and sleek.

- **What kind of international style speaks to me?** The charming cottage gardens of the British Isles? The quiet teahouses of Japan? The lush colors of Provence? The rough-and-tumble energy of the American Southwest? The kinds of landscapes and architecture you like can suggest themes for your own home. English and French country design fall under the "traditional" category; Asian looks can be exotic or contemporary; Southwestern styles are usually fairly rustic in character.

- **What colors do I like best—and in which combinations?** Soft greens? Saturated blue or pink? Rich red? Neutrals? Although your favorite style doesn't have to determine the color palette, there are some natural associations. A neutral palette, for example, can create a contemporary tableau, and hunter green—especially in combination with white furniture—has a more traditional look.

- **What kinds of foods do I cook most?** If you're a fan of fiery Latin or delicate Asian cuisine, you might want to eat in an exotic setting; the burger-and-dog crowd might feel more at home in a traditional venue.

FINDING YOUR STYLE

First, you'll need to get a firm sense of the look you want to give the space, and for that you should start with a little introspection. Go back to your idea file (see page 33) and have another look. Don't focus on the details, just the big picture—the elements that are repeated over and over. Does every page you chose feature a rustic stone fireplace? Or crisp, white-painted furniture? Low, simple furnishings and a Zen mood? Romantic Victorian wicker? Sleek stainless steel appliances? These repeated motifs will give you a good idea of the style you like best: traditional, contemporary, rustic, or exotic.

TIMELESS TRADITIONAL

Broad as it may be, "traditional" is a good descriptive term for most people's favorite decorating style. Traditional decor may mean anything from buttoned-up and formal to laid-back and casual; Chippendale or country; red, white, and blue, or, in French, *bleu, blanc,* and *rouge.* But basically, spaces with a traditional bent have some degree of symmetry, finished materials—wood with some kind of finish, painted or stained, or at least with a smooth surface; smooth stone; and so on—and a link to a particular historic genre, such as early American, French provincial, Italian country. Traditional furnishings are easy to find. Every outdoor furniture catalog and manufacturer offers a wide array of all-weather wicker, timeless teak, and aluminum furniture in classic shapes. This style is probably the most flexible—it's a cinch to spice up a largely traditional look with the addition of a few punchy, bright pillows or an exotic table setting—and the best suited to resale. Most people won't find a simple, classic kitchen offensive, whereas they might not appreciate your choice of a Polynesian hut. And if your house is traditional in style, and particularly if your outdoor kitchen and living areas are in close proximity to the house, traditional is the most appropriate way to go. A more overtly stylized look may well look out of place next to your shingled cottage or clapboard colonial.

Traditional design comes in a wide variety of forms. A few of the most characteristic follow:

CLASSICAL

The most formal version of traditional design is all about symmetry. Imagine the Parthenon, with its strict geometric lines and perfectly balanced decoration. An outdoor kitchen and living space with a classical look doesn't have to meet such a high standard, but you might want to incorporate details such as columns to support an overhead shelter, cabinetry with acanthus leaf carvings or fluting, limestone or granite surfaces, and wrought-iron furniture with scrolled arms and backrests.

AMERICANA

This look is what you'll find on front porches across the United States. Simple, comfortable furniture—think white rockers and comfortable wicker—and pretty upholstery in bright colors.

COUNTRY

Depending on which country you choose—the United States, France, Italy, Spain, or Mexico, to name a few—this style can vary widely. American country furnishings are fairly simple; Italian country can be a bit more ornate. Look for unpainted wood and fabrics printed in a traditional pattern.

If your house and garden have a traditional look, it's usually a good idea to match your furnishings and accessories to that style. This simple dining set has a charming country appeal that is in perfect keeping with the architecture of the porch that shelters it.

HOW TO GET THE TRADITIONAL LOOK

Love the traditional look? Here's how to make it your own.

- **Keep it simple.**
  Most traditional design is restrained, without too much ornamentation. Finish first. Choose wooden cabinetry with a painted or stained finish, and symmetrical detailing.

- **Remember the past.**
  Many traditional designs are related to a particular style from the past: classical, Victorian, or Arts and Crafts are a few examples of historic looks that feel traditional today.

- **Pick the right pattern.**
  Look for stripes, checks, solids, or simple florals.

- **Accessorize wisely.**
  Lanterns have a great traditional look, as does anything nautical in nature.

RUSTIC RULES

Picture a scene in nature: The colors are earthy—greens, grays, and browns—the texture is varied—velvety moss, crackly leaves, rough rock—the forms are irregular—craggy mountains meet rolling meadows—and there's movement everywhere—flowing water, waving reeds and branches. Now translate those natural images to your outdoor kitchen. It sounds harder than it is. Start with color. It's easy to work the hues of nature into your man-made designs. The simplest choice is natural wood. In a rustic kitchen—unlike one with a traditional bent—wood is left as close to its original form as possible. You might opt to top your island with slabs of wood that look newly sliced from a tree, with knots and irregular sides (all sealed with a marine-grade polyurethane,

of course, to protect it from the elements). Or you might face the island with half-round cedar logs with the bark left on. Whatever you choose, you'll be incorporating plenty of warm woody colors into your plan. Natural stone—any type—will add some green or gray touches. And you can always choose furnishings made from woven reeds or upholstered in the colors of earth, sea, or sky.

Using natural materials takes care of texture, as well. Instead of a high-gloss finish for stone surfaces, go with a honed top and leave the edges rough. Choose furnishings with a natural finish, too; metal furnishings come with pebbled finishes that work well with a rustic scheme. Instead of designing everything according to a regular, symmetrical plan, include some free-form shapes like those

Symmetry is often a hallmark of traditional design. From the neat kitchen garden to the arrangement of chairs and bench to the apple-filled hurricanes, this dining area demonstrates a pleasing attention to balance and harmony.

found in nature. A curving island, perhaps, or a patio that seems to fade into the surrounding landscaping, thanks to artfully placed boulders and garden beds. For movement, use landscaping elements like trailing vines and trees with arching branches, hang wind chimes, or install a small pond with a waterfall nearby.

BASIC INSTINCTS

Because rustic design has a strong connection to the earth, it gives you a good excuse to introduce some elements that are downright primitive. A table crafted from a tree stump would make a great conversation starter for a party, and a firepit has been attracting gatherers since time immemorial. Fire in general is an important element of a rustic living space, so strongly consider including a fireplace or firepit in addition to your cooking equipment. And choose a style that's rugged and natural looking, not smooth and refined.

For shelter and other permanent structures, exposed rough-hewn beams create instant rustic ambience, as do garden structures such as trellises hung with vines. Paving stones like slate or bluestone are more appropriate than brick, which has a more traditional look and feel. A general rule of thumb is to choose materials with irregular surfaces and lines, and this extends to the layout of the kitchen itself.

Instead of an angular L, think about an oval or arcing counter, some type of organic shape that will work in harmony with the lines of your house. Seating areas can be set up in circular patterns, too, as if everyone were sitting around an imaginary campfire—an arrangement that fosters intimacy and comfort. Choose lighting that flickers— gas fixtures, tiki torches, or masses of candles—to create an alluring campfire glow. And serve unfussy food and drink: grilled quesadillas, perfect steaks, and cold beer.

Natural materials—stone, wood, and metal— often dominate rustic designs. You can control the look by choosing the degree of finish on each material. Rough-finished stone and wood give the most rustic look, whereas more finely finished versions of the same materials impart a more elegant effect.

A rustic outdoor space needn't resemble a set from the TV western *Rawhide*. Rustic can have a certain rough elegance. Here's how:

• **Go *au naturel.***
Forgo finishes such as paint and stain. Choose woods like teak or redwood that weather naturally, and opt for honed finishes on stone surfaces.

• **Rough it.**
Select furniture with a slightly rough look. Instead of wicker, go with woven reeds—anything with a bold, natural texture. For fabric, choose something that shows its weave, such as linen.

• **Embrace change.**
True rustic settings show the passage of time. Water wears trails in rock, wind warps trees with its force. Allow the elements in your design to show a little weather as well: Copper will age to a mellow patina; teak will turn gray with age; terra-cotta pots often grow moss over time.

• **Get real.**
Make sure your rustic spaces are well coordinated with your landscaping plan. They should feel connected and integrated, not as if the patio ends here and the landscaping starts there. The transition should be indistinguishable.

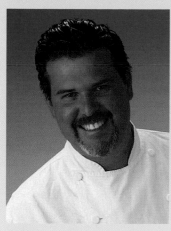

RICHARD SANDOVAL

Chef Richard Sandoval grew up in Mexico City and Acapulco, where his grandmother's home-style cooking and his restaurateur father instilled in him a lifelong love of fine food. After attending the prestigious Culinary Institute of America in Hyde Park, New York, Sandoval returned home to Acapulco, where he worked in his parents' restaurants, honing his craft and winning the National Toque D'Oro in 1992. In 1995, he opened his first restaurant in New York City, Savann, a traditional French restaurant, shortly followed by Savann East. But it was in 2001 with the opening of Maya, a "modern" Mexican restaurant also in New York City, that Sandoval's star began to rise. Soon he'd opened Tamayo and Zengo in Denver, Pampano in New York (with Placido Domingo), and TI in Las Vegas. He published his first cookbook, *Modern Mexican Flavors,* in 2003.

Professional Help

With restaurants all over the country, Chef Sandoval spends much of his time on the road—which makes his time at home in Southern California, with his wife and their two boys, all the more precious. "When I'm home I like simple things," he says. "I love to grill. I don't think there's anything better than being outdoors. And I like my kids to eat very healthily—the advantage with grilled food is that you don't have to use oils or butter." For cooking up his simple fare, Sandoval just completed a new outdoor kitchen. "I built it so I have all the components within my reach, so I don't have to go in to the [indoor] kitchen at all—I can just stay and talk to my guests."

The outdoor kitchen has an L-shape island, sealed limestone countertops, a 48" (1.2 m) grill with an infrared rotisserie, and a small refrigerator. "Next to my kitchen I built a patio with a dining area, so everyone can be together.

I usually do most of the cooking myself, but because I'm always cooking in my restaurants, when I invite people over I ask them to bring something. They're very diverse, so they each bring something from wherever they're from," he says. He also included a fireplace similar to a traditional Mexican chiminea in his design, but he chose one with a wood-burning oven on top. "In Mexico we do a lot of pit barbecue, so I like to cook in the chiminea. Sometimes I'll wrap things in banana leaves and cook them in the oven. And the fireplace is right in front of where my guests sit, so in cold times we can still sit out there."

The comfort of his guests was a prime concern for Sandoval. "We have a lot of family, and if you're going to cook for four you might as well cook for fifteen. Just make sure you set up enough space to make it comfortable so you can spread out your equipment." Another piece of advice for homeowners: "I think at the beginning, people might be afraid because building an outdoor kitchen can be pricy. But spend the extra money to get the better equipment—in the long run, you get what you pay for." And, practical as only a chef might be, Sandoval took steps to protect his own investment. "I had a special canvas—the kind they use to cover boats—made to cover each piece of equipment and preserve it from the elements."

CONTEMPORARY ARTS

A contemporary kitchen and living space is, in a way, the most difficult look to achieve. First, you want to create an effect that's sleek and clean, without looking cold and uncomfortable. Second, you have to be careful not to choose styles that will look dated in five years' time; an outdoor kitchen is a significant investment, and you want to enjoy it for many years to come. And third, because sleek simplicity defines contemporary design, you have to plan layout and storage extra carefully. Clutter will quickly ruin the lines of your contemporary space. That said, few things are as dramatic as a well-executed contemporary kitchen, full of gleaming stainless steel and interesting angles, and food looks particularly inviting set against a sparsely decorated dining area. So, if you have your heart set on a contemporary look, tread carefully and slowly. Take time to consult with an architect or designer (because the architecture won't be obscured by decorations, it's particularly important for contemporary spaces to have strong, striking "bones"). And choose your materials with an eye to practicality, certainly, but also to their subtle impact.

STEPS TO SUCCESS

To create a contemporary look, start by choosing the right materials. Stone, glass, stainless steel, and concrete are good choices. Keep the colors quiet overall, but consider including one brightly colored focal point—a red concrete countertop, say, or a cobalt tabletop. But overall, the look should be serene and peaceful, to keep the emphasis on the architecture and on the setting. You'll also want to make sure your contemporary outdoor living area meshes well with the surrounding landscaping, as well as your house. A modern patio and kitchen will look strange alongside a traditional house and a cottage garden; but most latter twentieth-century design will suit a sleek outdoor living area just fine. If you need to adjust your landscaping, simply go for a more angular, grid-like setup with minimal flowers, clipped hedges, abstract garden sculpture, and striking specimen plantings.

Creating an exotic look in your living space can be a wonderful excuse to exercise your sense of whimsy. There are no rules, and the sky's the limit in terms of creativity. A well-planned and—executed lighting scheme will create an inviting and intimate entertaining center. Note how the different types of lighting in this space—from lanterns to candles to firelight—work together to create a natural, comfortable ambiance.

Contemporary means sleek, simple, and modern—but it needn't be cold. Keep the look inviting and timeless by following these guidelines:

- **Attend to details.**
  Just because contemporary spaces are simple doesn't mean they have to be dull. Use details—such as stamped concrete floors or extra-thick countertop edges—to make a strong visual impact.

- **Use color.**
  Yes, white and stainless steel will give you that clean, contemporary look, so if that's what you want, you're all set. If

not, keep the forms neat and angular, but get creative with color. Consider integrally stained concrete in rich hues of red or orange; contemporary resin furniture with bright—even acid-hued—upholstery; or glass tiles in bright colors.

- **Think texture.**
  Keep shapes simple, but look for furnishings with interesting texture—woven vines or brushed metals, for example.

- **Include metal.**
  You can't go wrong with metal: stainless steel for countertops and appliances, shiny chrome faucets, and aluminum furniture.

Contemporary design can be warm and inviting, as demonstrated by this dramatic dining area. Though the materials—natural wood and stone—are typical of rustic style, the aesthetic here is pure contemporary, with a distinctive play between angles and curves, rough and smooth, inside and out.

Simple lines and sleek materials create a streamlined, contemporary look. Sticking to a warm color palette—terra cotta-hued tiles on the floor and counter and upholstery with bold red and orange stripes—helps to reinforce the southwestern style of this outdoor kitchen.

FOCUS ON: FURNITURE

Buying new outdoor furniture can be a significant investment. You want to choose timeless pieces that will stand up to the elements without a lot of maintenance. As you shop, you'll find a lot of different materials on the market. Here's what you need to know to make the right choice.

Wicker. Traditionally, "wicker" refers to furniture crafted from woven reeds, usually rattan, which should be sheltered under a porch roof. Today, various materials may be used, including extruded resin, vinyl, or fiberglass. All-weather wicker can be left outside year-round.

Wood. Look for sustainably harvested species, such as teak and jarrah, labeled "plantation grown." Though it's beautiful and classic, good quality wood furniture can be expensive and must be kept covered in the winter; even treated wood furniture will eventually degrade if left exposed to the elements for several years.

Resin. Plastic or polypropylene is lightweight, strong, colorfast, and fade resistant. Affordable and easy to care for, resin furniture does not have the timeless look of wicker or wood, and lesser quality pieces may not last long.

Wrought iron. Solid iron is forged into a wide variety of forms. Although it has an old-fashioned beauty, wrought iron can rust over time, and is heavy and difficult to rearrange.

Cast iron or aluminum. Molten metal is poured into molds to form solid frames that are lightweight, but with the look of heavier wrought iron.

Tubular. The metal frame is hollow and lightweight. Tubular metal furnishings have a casual, modern look that may not be suitable for a high-end or traditional setting.

Extruded Aluminum, resin, or steel. This material is pushed through a form to create a solid, malleable tube. Like tubular metal furnishings, extruded aluminum pieces can look modern, which may not be appropriate in some settings.

HOT TIPS

Architect Steve Straughan, a partner in the KAA Design Group in Los Angeles, has become a bit of an expert in the outdoor kitchen and living room in recent years. "There's not a home we're doing these days that doesn't have an outdoor room," he says.
A few pointers:

- **Size matters.** "Make sure it's wide enough to furnish comfortably. I've seen spaces that are too shallow to furnish. Eleven to twelve feet (3–3.5 m) in width is really the minimum dimension."

- **Stay warm.** "We incorporate heating into the architecture. In a covered outdoor room we recess electric heat in the ceiling, or if it's beamed or trellised, we'll mount heaters on the sides of the beams to hide them. Alternatively, though it's much more costly, we'll do radiant heating in the concrete floor slab."

- **Protect yourself.** "Wind can be an issue. We have a number of projects by the beach or facing west on a canyon, so we include outdoor curtains. You can close them if it's windy or too sunny. From a decorating standpoint, they create a really romantic look."

- **Be creative.** "We'll do things like fill the bottom of a gas fireplace with sand or broken glass, so the fire comes up through that material. All of our masonry fireplaces have a gas feed, even if it's used only as a starter."

EXOTIC AIRS

If you envision your outdoor living space as a getaway, an escape from the more everyday rituals of indoor life, then the exotic look is for you. After all, what better antidote to the status quo than a setting that looks like a scene from *Arabian Nights* or the musical *South Pacific?* And it's easier than you might imagine to inject an element of the exotic into your suburban landscape. First, start with an idea. Think back to a great vacation and write down the details of the restaurant you loved or the beachside shack where you ate lunch. Or flip through some travel magazines and tear out the pictures that speak to you. Identify the details of those images you like. A low table with cushions instead of chairs? Romantic, arched ceilings and twisting columns? A tented roof? Once you have a sense of the look you'd like to achieve, decide how much or how little you want to devote to creating it. For example, will you be happy with Polynesian-style furnishings and tabletop accessories, or do you need your own grass hut? If you opt for the latter, keep in mind that the next owners of your house might not share your enthusiasm for island architecture. For resale purposes, you might want to contain your exotic flair to removable items.

STEPS TO SUCCESS

Because an exotic look is usually a fairly personal style, it's generally best to keep the exotic elements in the outdoor kitchen fairly subtle. You might, for example, talk to your architect about working some Moorish arches into the roofline, or use Spanish clay tiles instead of traditional shingles. These are elements that can later work well with a future owner's more traditional style. In terms of materials, go for subtle touches that speak—but don't scream— "exotic": concrete counters with shells or semiprecious stones mixed in, or cabinet hardware with a handmade, ethnic look. Tile, available in myriad colors and patterns, is a natural element for adding exotic flair—a few minutes shopping on the Internet will turn up traditionally Italian, Spanish, and North African looks, just to name a few.

Want to create a look reminiscent of a tropical grass hut? Keep the materials in the same color family—here blond wood furnishings match the material of the enclosure—use woven accessories, such as the light fixtures shown, and choose tropical floral prints for upholstery. After a few daiquiris, your guests will think they're in Anguilla.

Creating an outdoor living space with exotic flair is easy—just relax and let yourself have fun.

• Think "escape."

An exotic room will spirit you away to another place and time, so spare no detail. First think of the architecture, then extend the style to the furnishings and accessories.

• Use color.

Exotic design often features strong colors. Think of the colors of sun and sand, sky and water: rich reds, oranges, and pinks; turquoise and teal; and touches of gold and silver.

• Material matters.

Natural materials are usually a key feature of exotic design. So, instead of synthetic surfacing and shiny metals, opt for slightly rough-textured woods and stones, grass, and bamboo.

INSIDE OUT

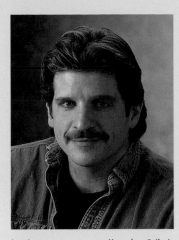

JOHN STAGE

These days, when John Stage feels like hitting the road, it's to ride his motorcycle along the Hudson River from his home in New York City to Syracuse or Rochester, where two of his three restaurants are located. But it wasn't so long ago that he and two friends spent five years on the open road, cooking up barbecue in a 55-gallon (208 l) drum they'd converted into a portable grill before they opened the first Dinosaur Bar-B-Que in Syracuse, in 1983. Not long after that, they doubled their space, and then opened a second outpost in Rochester. Finally, in 2004, Stage opened his third restaurant, in New York City—a setting that poses some regulatory challenges when it comes to cooking over an open flame, but one that's proving to be wildly popular among barbecue-starved locals. Stage published his first cookbook in 2001.

Professional Help

Like many of us, Stage has limited space for his outdoor kitchen. "I have a very small backyard," he says, "but the size doesn't really matter as long as you're very organized with your space—you can produce the same results with a little hibachi as you can with a huge grill. It's just a matter of what you know and how you plan." His advice is to design your cooking space so that you have everything at your fingertips, "so you're not running around like crazy." Like any good chef, Stage relies on his *mise en place*, a carefully orchestrated lineup of ingredients arranged before cooking begins. "Set up your ingredients on a side table so you won't have to run inside every time you need something," he says. Another key tip: "Know your fire." Stage believes it's possible to achieve high-quality results on an inexpensive kettle grill, as long as you take care to build your fire correctly. "Use a two-tier heat system, with a high pile of coals on one side and a low pile on the other—that way you can control how much fire your food is getting." What's Stage's favorite thing to cook at home? With his long hours at the restaurant, he relies on quick-and-easy meals such as dry-aged sirloin steaks, instead of the slow-cooked barbecue that made him famous.

When it comes to furnishings and decorations, however, give yourself a free rein. An outdoor living space is the ideal place to express your whimsical side, so take a creative approach to every aspect. Choose new or antique furnishings that give your space a strong international flavor—a low teak table for an Asian look or one with a mosaic top for a Moroccan effect. Fabric is a great way to reinforce the theme. Though there are many beautiful all-weather fabrics on the market today, don't feel limited to outdoor materials.

If your living space is sheltered, you can furnish it like an indoor room; if it's *en plein air,* you can take pillows inside when necessary. Table settings are another easy, inexpensive way to create an exotic atmosphere. Look for flatware with interesting handle designs, napkins with beaded trim, unique napkin rings, and handmade plates and glasses. Lighting—lanterns with colored glass, torches, candles—will finish the scene with an alluring glow.

CHAPTER FIVE

SECRETS OF SUCCESS
IT'S IN THE DETAILS

Have you ever looked at a beautiful room in a magazine—or in a friend's home—and wondered what exactly sets it apart from the run-of-the-mill spaces in which most of us live? Aside from tricks of photo stylists, successful designers use a number of secrets to craft rooms that are as attractive as they are livable. For interior rooms, designer know-how includes furniture arrangement, color theory, understanding of scale and texture, lighting, climate control, and more. When it comes to exterior spaces, the keys to a top-notch cooking and living space are much the same, just applied slightly differently. Yes, you can set up a grill and a rolling cart and call it an outdoor kitchen. You can put a table and chairs on your patio and call it your outdoor dining room. But these makeshift arrangements will fall far short of the comfortable living spaces of your dreams. To turn those dreams into reality, you need to consider the nitty-gritty, less-than-romantic elements behind every successful outdoor space—topics such as lighting, weather protection, cleaning, and even pests. Take care to address all these important issues, and you'll find yourself with a living space in which you'll really want to live.

A truly successful outdoor kitchen has it all: a great location, the right equipment, comfortable hangout areas, beautiful materials, and details that make it your own.

SOLAR POWER

As you plan your outdoor lighting, consider an attractive alternative to low-voltage fixtures: solar-powered lights. These fixtures are equipped with a solar panel that uses the sun's rays to charge the fixture's internal battery, automatically turning the lights on at dusk and off at daybreak. These environmentally friendly fixtures don't require any cables, so they're the easiest installation option out there—and you can move them any time you want. Just keep in mind that they require approximately eight hours of sunlight every day to work effectively.

LIGHTING YOUR WAY

It may not be the first thing you thought about when you decided to build an outdoor kitchen, but lighting is one of the single most important design elements, both from practical and aesthetic standpoints. First of all, without proper lighting, it's difficult to cook: How can you tell when your chicken reaches that fleeting brown-but-not-yet black stage if you're grilling in near darkness? Second, unlit patio areas and paths are dangerous to navigate. And third, the right lighting fixtures will emphasize your property value, pointing out beautiful architecture, highlighting garden beds at night, and adding valuable decorative detail. In fact, in an outdoor space where there's little opportunity for the decorative trappings of indoor rooms, lighting fixtures offer a prime chance to introduce a touch of drama, sophisticated elegance, or rustic charm.

The types of light fixtures you choose will depend on the style of your house and outdoor living space, and on the activities that will take place in the area. Here, a lantern affixed to the wall creates a soft pool of light, and fixtures on the ground direct light up toward the pergola, highlighting the architecture.

The best outdoor lighting plans use fixtures both for their illumination and their decorative impact. Here, bold fixtures—hanging lanterns inside the living area stand up to the strong architectural lines of the space.

Now that you understand the importance of good outdoor lighting, you'll need a lighting plan. Think about how you'll use the space and what you want the lights to achieve. Start with task lighting—directed light designed to illuminate specific activities such as cooking. Consider your workspace. Do you need to light a large work area, or just a grill? Keep in mind that you want the light to shine in front of you (many homes have a spotlight mounted on the wall of the house, fruitlessly illuminating the cook's back as he or she stands in front of a grill set out from the house). Next, think about ambient lighting—the soft, overall illumination that creates atmosphere. It's a good idea to plan ambient lighting around dining and living areas, so guests can see their food and each other. Then, plan path lighting. You should illuminate all pathways, as well as stairways and the edges of raised decks. Finally, accent lighting can highlight particular features such as a statue at the end of the pool or a spectacular planting.

Pathway and accent lights are frequently low-voltage fixtures, which use a transformer to convert household current into safe, energy-efficient, low-voltage current. Unlike traditional line voltage lights (the kind used indoors), you need only to dig a shallow trench for the low-voltage cables, so you won't disturb a mature landscaping plan. Many transformers come equipped with a timer and photo cell, so you can set the lights to turn on at a particular time of day—dusk, for example. Low-voltage fixtures come in a wide range of styles, from simple and utilitarian to positively whimsical.

WEATHER REPORT

If you've ever flipped burgers with cold rain dripping down your neck or monitored the ribs while wiping the sweat from your brow as the sun beat down on your scalp, you know that the elements are the natural enemy of the

RICK BROWNE

Being an award-winning photojournalist has given Rick Browne ample opportunity to taste barbecue all over the world, but his specialty is good old American 'cue. He's the creator, host, and executive producer of the PBS television show *Barbecue America,* and the author of four cookbooks on the subject, including *The Barbecue America Cookbook,* published in 2004. He travels all over the country judging some of the biggest barbecue competitions around and holds the prestigious Ph.B. degree (Doctor of Barbecue Philosophy) from the Kansas City Barbecue Society. Browne's latest project, *Ready, Aim, Grill,* a cooking show for hunters and fishermen, debuted on the Outdoor Channel in July.

Professional Help

Like many homeowners, Rick Browne has cooked for years on a grill on his deck, but this barbecue aficionado and cookbook author is finally ready for, as he puts it, "something a little more permanent." Browne and his wife are in the process of building a new outdoor kitchen on a patio behind their Vancouver, Washington, home. "We're putting in a really nice (grill) island with a gazebo-type roof. It's in a Pacific Northwest style, with big timbers and natural stone," says Browne. The roof is a necessity in rainy Washington state, and one that will extend the outdoor cooking season to nearly year-round— "We'll use it eighty percent of the year," he says—and the roof will make the space more comfortable for his family and friends. "No one wants to sit outside if there's hot sun beaming down on them," he says, "so it's important to plan some kind of shade." But although Browne's kitchen will be outfitted with a 36" (91.5 cm) gas grill, a refrigerator, a warming drawer, a large sink, and an island, he advises others planning an outdoor kitchen to fit their new space to their own particular needs. "I cook more than the average person," he notes. "I write cookbooks and test recipes for sponsors, but when you're designing your own kitchen you should plan something that fits your lifestyle. Don't go crazy and get a 52" (132 cm)-wide grill if there's two of you and you rarely entertain."

outdoor cook. But they don't have to be—if you plan carefully. Now, no amount of planning in the world will make you want to spend time outside during extreme bad weather, but a well-executed outdoor living space will offer comfortable respite from light rain, wind, cold, and heat. Planning a sheltered outdoor living area does add expense, however. So, if your budget is tight, your weather-protection plans may need to end at the beginning: Set your grill outside your kitchen door, under the overhang of your roof, and take the food inside to eat during inclement weather. On sunny days, sit under an umbrella. On cold nights, wear a sweater. If your finances allow a little more latitude, plan for every condition, with shelter from the rain and wind—both for you and your equipment—and protection from the cold.

GIVE ME SHELTER

The most obvious way to protect yourself and your guests from wet and windy weather is to build a covered outdoor kitchen. Most outdoor kitchens attached to the house have some sort of roof, and you have a number of ways to proceed. One option would be to build a summer kitchen, with a traditional shed roof and open or partially open walls, perhaps with knee walls and half-columns. Or you might plan a simple roof held up by columns—a sort of carport for your kitchen area. A loggia is a more elegant approach and a lovely way to add architectural distinction to your house and its outdoor living spaces. For a stand-alone space, you might erect a peaked roof above the outdoor kitchen, or place the cooking area inside a gazebo. For all these options, you'll need to invest in high-quality roofing materials, just

The best protection against the elements is a completely enclosed roof structure, such as the one shown here. The space still feels like part of the outdoors because the sides are open, the materials are rustic, and the decorations are natural. A built-in hutch displays a personal collection.

CHOICES, CHOICES

Once you start shopping for lighting fixtures, you'll find a wide variety of styles and shapes available. A few common options and their best applications follow:

Low-voltage and solar fixtures Available in many styles from simple globes to delicate tulip-shape forms, these are most appropriate for use as accent and path lighting.

Sconces Wall-mounted fixtures are ideal for installation on either side of a doorway or anywhere you want to add ambient lighting in a covered area.

Lanterns Hung from a ceiling or even a sturdy tree branch, lanterns lend a romantic touch. For an authentic statement, look for gas-lit lanterns, which give an old-fashioned New Orleans–style flicker.

Pendants A good choice for task lighting above a covered kitchen area, pendants come in a wide range of styles and sizes. A pair or trio will light an island or bar nicely.

Spotlights Indispensable workhorses of outdoor lighting, spotlights point direct task lighting—or accent lighting—wherever you need it. A combination of utilitarian spotlights and more decorative fixtures will create a practical, attractive lighting scheme.

Torches Electric, candle, gas, or kerosene torches lend an exotic air to living and dining areas.

Candles Masses of candles impart romance like nothing else. Candlesticks or holders are a great way to introduce a personal decorative touch into your outdoor living space.

as you would for your home. Consider the doors between the outdoor room and your home. If the outdoor space is connected to an indoor living room, sliding pocket doors, which are concealed inside the walls of the house when open, offer the most flexibility: When they're open the line between indoors and out disappears entirely, or open just one for a more enclosed feel, or close off the outdoor room completely. Skylights can introduce more sunlight into the space, if necessary.

Alternatively, you might opt for a trellis or pergola-style shelter, with open beams wound with heavy vines. This setup offers a bit less protection but creates a romantic, natural look that links indoor and outdoor living areas nicely—at a very cost-effective price. (For information on building an arbor, see page 142.)

TO PROTECT AND TO SERVE

After you've spent significant time and money buying appliances and fixtures for your outdoor kitchen, it would be a shame to leave them to the mercy of the elements. Over time, even the most expensive all-stainless-steel grill will display the ravages of rain and wind (especially if you live near the ocean, where salt air will slowly pit any metal). Fortunately, you can keep your kitchen running smoothly—and looking terrific—by taking a few simple precautions. Sheltering the kitchen with a roof, as discussed earlier, is your first line of defense against rain and wind. But just as important—and all-important if you won't be covering the kitchen—is a cover for each piece of equipment. Any home center or hardware store will stock a number of vinyl grill covers, most likely in various sizes and weights—the heavier, the better. Look for a model with hooked-fabric tabs on the side to cinch the cover around the grill so wind won't blow it—and your grill—across your yard. A quick Internet search will reveal fancier cover designs; you might even find one emblazoned with the logo of your favorite sports team.

Covering auxiliary elements such as a separate burner, oven, warming drawer, refrigerator, and sink, can be a bit more difficult. A tarp and some bungee cords will do the trick effectively, if not attractively: Just lash the tarp around the island when you're done cooking, or, if you're working at a counter attached to the wall of your house, install some hooks on the wall and use the grommets in the tarp to attach it tightly. If you're handy with a sewing machine—or know someone who is—you might opt to fashion custom covers for your equipment from marine-grade vinyl, the kind that's used on boats.

A sheltered outdoor kitchen will protect you and your equipment from wind, rain, and sun—an important consideration both in terms of your comfort and your investment. Of course, building an enclosure like this one, which requires a foundation, supports, and a roof, is significantly more expensive than installing an uncovered kitchen.

Accessories such as utensils, cutting boards, and small appliances should always be tucked away inside an enclosed cabinet or drawer when not in use.

KEEPING WARM

If you want to use your outdoor room when the temperature drops, plan ahead by including a heating system. Portable, outdoor-rated space heaters are widely available, and although not the most attractive option—the largest and most effective ones look a bit like stainless-steel lamp posts—they are portable and affordable. For a less dominant look, table-top heaters can add a little warmth on chilly evenings. In a sheltered living space, electric heat mounted on the ceiling or radiant heat inside the concrete slab beneath the paving will keep things cozy, even on the coolest day. But for atmosphere, nothing beats the look and feel of a burning fire.

Outdoor fireplaces come in an array of styles, from prefabricated gas or wood-burning units that can be built into a custom surround to completely custom-made concrete or brick pizza ovens. A firepit, which can be either dug into the ground or fully portable, or a Mexican-style chiminea are other attractive, cozy, and less-expensive options. When using one of these portable wood burners, make sure you keep it a safe distance from combustible materials. And for convenience's sake, it can be a good idea to build a storage compartment into your outdoor living area for storing wood, newspaper, and other supplies.

CARE AND HANDLING

Because cleaning is the last thing most of us wants to do indoors or out, it is smart to take care to make your outdoor kitchen as low maintenance and easy to clean as possible. That means choosing surfacing materials with an eye to their upkeep, as well as their function and style. For a truly low-maintenance workspace, for instance, you probably wouldn't choose ceramic tile as your surfacing material. For all its beauty and durability, ceramic tile has an undisputable Achilles' heel: the grout lines, which—even when sealed with a penetrating acrylic sealer—seem to be a magnet for dirt and grime. If you love the look of tile, limit

If your kitchen is attached to your house, you can build a porch-type shelter for it, supported by columns. This one has strong architectural beams running across its width, creating a nice contrast to the brick house and patio paving.

FOCUS ON: COLD-CLIMATE CUISINE

Outdoor kitchens are not just a warm-climate phenomenon. Far from it: Today, homeowners from Minnesota to Montana to Maine are enjoying the rewards of outdoor cooking and living. But planning an outdoor room in a cold climate has its challenges. Plumbing, for example, becomes more complicated because pipes must be insulated, buried beneath the frost line, and wrapped with heated wire where the pipe emerges from the ground to prevent freezing. Of course, many homeowners simply opt to simplify things by making running water a summer-only convenience, hooking a garden hose to the faucet when climate allows. The main goal is for the cook and guests to stay warm when temperatures drop. Fall in the Adirondacks can be downright frigid, as can spring in the Midwest, so even if you're not planning to grill in the dead of winter you'll want to plan for some heating if you expect to cook outside for more than one season.

its use to the backsplash or other vertical areas, where it will be less likely to accumulate dirt.

Your two best surfacing options, maintenance-wise, are probably stainless steel or granite. Stainless steel is impervious to moisture, hygienic, and more resistant than most surfacing materials to the ravages of salty sea air. Granite has some surface imperfections, so it's not quite as hygienic as stainless steel, but it's still a hard, tough surface that won't stain or scratch. You can also set hot pots and

An outdoor fireplace is one way to stay warm in cold weather. You can choose wood-burning or gas-fueled models—or a combination of the two: a wood-burning fireplace with a gas igniter.

RAIN, RAIN, GO AWAY

Sometimes, despite your best efforts to outwit the weather, the skies will open up and pour on your son's graduation cookout or your Friday-night neighborhood barbecue. If you've planned your kitchen well, you'll be high and dry while you cook, even if you do end up eating inside. But if your setup is bare bones, you'll just have to grin and bear it. Do take some precautions, however. Never use anything electric (an electric charcoal starter, for instance) in wet conditions. And watch your step: Wooden decks can become treacherous when slicked with rain or snow. Keep your bad-weather grilling to a minimum. Cook side dishes inside so you won't have to stand outdoors tending multiple courses.

utensils directly on its surface without worrying about burn marks. Concrete is another good option, though not quite as tough as some might imagine. Unless you use an acrylic sealant on concrete—which changes the smooth, leathery surface many homeowners love—it is somewhat porous; acids such as vinegar and wine can stain it; hot pots will burn the surface; and sunlight may change the color of integrally stained concrete. Water, on the other hand, will not warp or mar the material.

When it comes to cleaning up at the end of each meal, your sponge will glide more smoothly over seamless countertops, and an undermounted sink makes it easy to wipe crumbs right into the sink (and eliminates the grime-trapping rim where a traditional sink meets the countertop).

Maintenance and durability are key considerations for more than just surfacing. The sides, or walls, of most grill islands and counters will be constructed from either concrete block or plywood and 2 x 4 (5 x 10 cm) framework, topped with concrete backer board, to which the finish materials are fixed. Finish materials include—but are not limited to—stucco, stone, wood, and tile. Of these options, wood is probably the least durable because it's prone to shrinking, expanding, and cracking as temperature and humidity levels shift. If, on the other hand, you opt for

stucco, stone, or tile facing material, moisture damage will be a much less pressing concern. In fact, you can hose down your outdoor kitchen periodically, assuming cabinet doors and drawer fronts fit snugly.

CLEANUP TIME

Keeping your outdoor kitchen clean is as easy as knowing the best way to clean each material.

STAINLESS STEEL SURFACES, SINKS, AND CABINETRY

Wash stainless steel with a gentle detergent—such as dish detergent—or a solution of baking soda and water. Avoid scouring powders or steel wool, which will scratch stainless steel and, over time, can remove the hard oxide coating that makes stainless steel "stainless." Dry with a paper towel or soft cloth. To shine a sink, polish it with a cloth dipped in vinegar, or rub with mineral oil to remove streaks.

Even the most high-end, elegant outdoor kitchen should be designed with easy maintenance in mind. Tough materials such as stainless steel, stone, and tile make this kitchen a cinch to wipe and hose clean after meals.

For a truly low-maintenance outdoor kitchen, choose sturdy surfacing materials such as stainless steel for appliances and counters and concrete or stucco for the walls of the grill island.

PORCELAIN SINKS

Clean with a mild detergent and sponge or nylon scrubber. Do not use abrasive cleansers, which can damage the porcelain enamel coating on the cast-iron sink.

CONCRETE COUNTERTOPS

Use a mild, nonabrasive cleanser, such as dish detergent and a sponge or nylon scrubbing pad.

GRANITE

Wash with mild soap or use a commercial granite cleanser (available through stone-supply showrooms and home centers).

CERAMIC TILE

Wash with warm water and dish detergent. Grout lines may need extra attention, such as scrubbing with a toothbrush and a weak solution of household bleach.

CLUTTER CONTROL

Your low-maintenance kitchen will look neat and clean only if you've planned enough storage to keep clutter to a minimum. Just as you do inside, make sure there's a place for everything—so everything can go into its place. A drawer for spices and oils and another for utensils will keep counters free. Cabinet space for small appliances, bowls, and other equipment makes it easy to put everything away

CLEANING THE GRILL

For peak performance, it's essential to maintain your grill according to the manufacturer's specifications. A few general guidelines follow:

Exterior care. For a stainless steel grill, clean with a solution of soap and water or baking soda and water. Never use an abrasive cleanser. If grease or carbon buildup has stained the housing, use a soft brush to scrub gently. You may need to use a degreaser or a sodium hydroxide cleanser to dissolve the crystallized carbon. Read the product brochure, or contact the manufacturer or its website for cleaning suggestions for removing baked-on dirt.

Interior care. Brush the grates before and after each use to minimize the need for major cleaning. Do not immerse the grates in water; instead, use a wet wire-bristle brush on them when the grates are cold. You can clean stainless steel grates with an abrasive pad or sponge and dish detergent. Burner elements are slightly more sensitive. Residue and drippings from meat or marinades can clog the burner holes. Spiders sometimes pose another problem, nesting inside the burner or valve. Because clogged burners can cause dangerous flare-ups, it's important to remove the burners periodically for cleaning. Use a brush to clean out all the holes and the valve, then flush with a hose to make sure all the holes are clear. Discourage spiders by firing up the grill periodically between uses.

Stainless steel, stucco, and tile are good options for outdoor kitchens. Many professional kitchen designers will specify only stainless steel; they feel that appliances made from other materials just don't stand the test of time.

Despite its rough-and-ready appearance, stainless steel does require some care. Regular cleaning and oiling will protect it over the long haul. Invest in a sturdy cover to protect a freestanding grill when it's not in use.

at the end of the meal, leaving counters open when not in use. It can also be a good idea to install a rack on the backsplash for hanging often-used utensils (some ventilation hoods have built-in racks) and even a magnetic knife strip. (If children play nearby, keep knives in a locked drawer.) When your supplies are nearby, but off of the counter, it's much easier to keep your work surfaces clean and neat.

UNWANTED VISITORS

Whether you live in a manicured suburban neighborhood or an isolated wooded setting, chances are good that at some time you'll have to deal with common backyard pests: insects, rodents, stray dogs and cats, raccoons, skunks, and even bears. These animals are all drawn to food, so when you're planning an outdoor kitchen it's crucial that you make sure it's less attractive to animals than it is to you.

BEAR NECESSITIES

With shrinking woodlands, today even neighborhood backyards near wooded areas can attract the occasional hungry bear. To prevent such a visit, remove anything that a bear might want to investigate: birdseed, fallen fruit, garbage cans, a dirty grill, or a grill grease-collection can. Store garbage in a sealed container; if you've seen bears in your area, invest in a bear-proof garbage can. If you see a bear, stay calm and far away. If you are in a residential area, call your local animal control board (see the government pages of your phone book). If you are near a park, call the park ranger to remove the bear. Alternatively, from a very safe distance (an upstairs window or balcony), make a lot of frightening noise—bang pots and pans, blow a horn, shout—so the bear won't feel welcome. You can also purchase an infrared body heat and motion detector that emits ear-piercing sounds and flashing lights if an animal (bear, raccoon, dog, or deer) enters its 40' (12 m) field of "vision." Another motion-detecting device shoots a high-pressure blast of water in a full circle—sold in garden supply departments, stores, and catalogs—for repelling smaller pests like neighborhood cats, dogs, opossums, and raccoons (see Resources, page 156).

FOOD SAFETY

Whether you're cooking inside or out, your and your guests' health relies on the cleanliness of your workspace. To eliminate bacteria in your outdoor kitchen, follow these easy steps:

Wash your hands. Clean your hands before and after handling food and in between jobs—especially after cutting up raw chicken or meat, and before slicing fruit or plating and serving food.

Rinse fruits and vegetables. Remove surface dirt with a brush if necessary before cutting them up to cook or serve raw.

Clean cutting boards. Wash with hot, soapy water and dry with paper towels. Periodically sanitize with a solution of 1 teaspoon (5 ml) bleach per 1 quart (1 l) of water. Rinse and dry with paper towels.

Keep all surfaces, utensils, towels, and sponges clean. Immediately wash anything that has come in contact with raw meat. Better yet, keep a separate sponge and cutting board reserved for meat and chicken to avoid cross contamination.

RODENTS

No one likes to think about them, but rodents such as mice, squirrels, and chipmunks are attracted to food and to warm, cozy places to build their nests. The best thing you can do to keep rodents away from your outdoor kitchen is to eliminate any access to cabinet interiors, and take care never to leave food—even tiny scraps or crumbs—out in the open. This includes bird food and pet food. Also eliminate any sources of standing or dripping water near an outdoor kitchen: birdbaths, dripping spigots, and so on.

RACCOONS AND SKUNKS

These nocturnal marauders can make a mess of your garbage, ripping standard cans open and digging through the contents in search of something to eat. The first thing to try is a well-sealed garbage container, like a bear-proof can (see "Bear Necessities"). Or, you can purchase an odorless spray with an unpleasant taste that, when sprayed on garbage and garbage containers, will deter subsequent

If biting insects are a big concern in your area, consider positioning your outdoor kitchen inside a screened porch. Just take extra care when it comes to ventilating the space. It may be a good idea to consult with a design professional to ensure proper air circulation.

visitors. Raccoons can be carriers of rabies, so never get too close, and if you see one of these nocturnal animals during the day, call a wildlife agent to trap it.

INSECTS

Two types of insects can make your time outside less than pleasant: biting insects, such as mosquitoes and yellow jackets, and bacteria-spreading insects, such as cluster flies. A number of insect control options are available, some more effective than others. One choice is a "bug zapper," a lantern-shaped device often hung in a tree. A zapper consists of an insect-attracting fluorescent light surrounded by electrified wire mesh. As the insect flies toward the light, it hits the mesh and is instantly vaporized. These units are, unfortunately, not effective against mosquitoes, which are not attracted to the fluorescent light. Never hang these traps near a seating or eating area, because when they "zap" an insect, they can release bacteria into the air. Insect traps are a better bet for outdoor living spaces. There are special electric or propane-powered traps available that emit a combination of mosquito-attractive octenol, carbon dioxide, moisture, and sometimes warmth, luring the mosquitoes and then vacuuming them into a disposable net where they die. These traps cover an area of a third of an acre or more and are effective if run throughout the season, because after the local females are killed, there will be no future generations. Simple, disposable pheromone traps that target various insect pests can be hung in trees to lure and trap insects and can be replaced as needed (see Resources, page 156). If you're installing a mister to cool your patio area, you can find models that incorporate a safe pesticide into the mist. Or, opt for a personal insect repellent on your clothing and citronella candles or torches placed strategically around the living space. You should also take steps to eliminate standing water on your property; pools and puddles are breeding grounds for mosquitoes— even water standing in a flowerpot saucer, because these pests can lay eggs in as little as $\frac{1}{4}$" (0.5 cm) of water. One very attractive mosquito "trap" is a small, decorative fish pond—mosquitoes will land on the surface of the water to lay eggs, only to be snapped up and eaten by goldfish or special, small "mosquito" fish that you can buy at pond stores. To avoid attracting bees, do not wear flowery perfume and pink or red clothing (nectar-flower colors) when in the yard during the day. You'll also find various repellent products on the market to make your job easier; just be sure to read the labels to ensure that these products are safe to use around food, pets, and children.

HOT TIPS

Larry Malesky, sales manager of the Fireplace & Barbecue Design Center in Coconut Creek, Florida, has noticed a new way of looking at outdoor cooking spaces. "It's no longer just a barbecue area," he says. "It's a 'summer kitchen.'" To help his clients plan the outdoor cooking and living spaces they want, Malesky sticks to the following principles:

- **What's right for you?** "Think about your cooking habits and whether you'll be entertaining," he says. This exercise will help you decide what kind of outdoor kitchen you need.

- **Grill size.** "The next thing to consider is the size of the grill," he notes. "Base it on the size of your family. A 20" or 30" (51 or 76-cm) -wide grill is fine for a family of five."

- **Location.** "You have to incorporate traffic patterns," he says. "In terms of location, you don't want to block out window views from the house."

- **Care.** "The only truly 'stainless' steel," says Malesky, "is surgical-grade steel, but that's not strong enough for a grill or cabinetry, so the stainless steel used in outdoor kitchen products is reinforced with nickel or steel, which will rust or pit over time. To protect it, wipe down surfaces that don't come into contact with food once a week with stainless steel cleaner or WD-40." (Wipe counter surfaces with nontoxic mineral oil.)

CHAPTER SIX

BUYER'S GUIDE
PRODUCT RECOMMENDATIONS
FOR EFFICIENCY AND COMFORT

You've thought about everything from location to layout, windscreens to sunscreens. Now's the fun part: outfitting your outdoor kitchen with the appliances, materials, furniture, and accessories that will make it your own. You'll find yourself with a wide array of shopping venues. Home centers are a great place to look for a grill as well as accessories like ceiling fans and even furnishings. Dedicated barbecue stores—which often double as hearth-product showrooms in winter months—will have employee experts in the brands they sell, and many may let you try before you buy. And don't forget the Internet: Shopping around online can save time and money. Just remember to include shipping prices when you figure your savings. Here, we've gathered a sampling of the innovative, attractive outdoor kitchen products on the market. Have a look—hopefully they will entice you to begin your own shopping.

NOW YOU'RE COOKING

The **Vermont Castings** VC53505BI grill has a roomy cooking surface and professional-caliber quality, without too much bulk.

If you like to cook seafood, a setup like the Gourmet Fry Kit from **Masterbuilt** will give you the power you need, when you need it.

The optional rotisserie shown here on the **Vermont Castings** VCS4000 gas grill is great for roasting whole birds evenly without requiring constant attention.

The GJK2 Optimum gas grill from **MHP** offers 54,000 Btus of cooking power and 920 square inches (2,337 cm) of cooking space, plus an 18,000-Btu side burner, swing-away warming rack, and side table.

An Australian-style portable like the **Aussie** 11,000-Btu two-burner gas grill, with wheels and folding legs, is great for several steaks for a party.

The **Coleman** Backhome Select 7700 Grill has luxury extras, such as a rotisserie and even a fryer, steamer, warmer basket.

Ask your contractor about building a custom pizza oven like this one, which was designed by concrete designer **Tom Ralston**.

Outdoor-rated stainless steel **Lasertron** cabinetry has a sleek, modern look, but you can also go retro or traditional with this material.

For the convenience of more than one refrigerator and cabinet unit, check out high-end grill manufacturers like *Viking*.

For outdoor parties, a "keg-erator" chilling unit from *Vintage* is a party-friendly addition to your bar setup.

The elegant *Kamado* ceramic barbeque is a smoker, a grill, and oven. For versatility and visual appeal, it's a worth-while investment.

An undercounter refrigerator like this one from *KitchenAid* reduces trips to the kitchen, especially if you keep it stocked with condiments and favorite drinks.

You can never have too much ice during a summer party. Consider installing a dedicated ice maker, like the *Marvel* H296.

WHAT'S UNDER FOOT?

Available in four colors, 800 Toscano floor tile from **Ceramiche Fontana Bismantova** has the look of ancient terra-cotta but the durability and low maintenance of ceramic tile.

Using the same paving inside and out blurs the lines between interior and exterior living spaces. Geostone tile from **Edimax** is durable and frost-resistant.

This stunning concrete design from **Concrete Network** adds instant panache to a simple patio.

Paving is important in terms of function and decor. This simple, swirling pattern is colored concrete, by **Colorado Hardscapes**.

Add a spark of color to your deck or patio with weather-resistant rugs in Green Hopscotch, Green Rally, Terra-Cotta Hopscotch, or Terra-Cotta Rally, from **Plow & Hearth**.

Just hose down these easy-care indoor/outdoor rugs from **Plow & Hearth** made from fast-drying polypropylene.

It looks like sisal, but this long-wearing rug from **Plow & Hearth** is made of weather and stain-resistant polypropylene.

ILLUMINATING IDEAS

Decorative lights like these from **Plow & Hearth** give a porch or gazebo a romantic nighttime look—or string them from the trees, for an enchanted garden effect.

Hang tea lights in **Patio Companion's** Magnolia lanterns for an instant trip to fairyland.

Outdoor lighting comes in many forms, including this pretty table lamp from **Shady Lady**.

These "candles" from **Plow & Hearth** are actually rechargeable. Each set of four burns for 15 hours on a full charge.

These windproof outdoor luminaries from **Orvis** have paraffin candles that can withstand winds up to 20 mph. The stands and snuffer are durable black powder-coated iron.

This Moravian Star lighting fixture from **Plow & Hearth** has a beautiful antique brass finish and weatherproof channeling, for a carefree take on an indoor classic.

Weatherproof outdoor lamps from **Plow & Hearth** are constructed with powder-coated steel bases that are heavily weighted for stability.

HAVE A SEAT

Designed by interior designer and HGTV host Joe Ruggiero, the Chelsea collection from *Terra* is appropriate indoors and out.

The **Bristol** Gate-Leg table is versatile: fully extended, it seats four; folded once it becomes a console; folded twice it measures just 8" (20.5 cm) wide.

The Lily Love Seat from **Maine Cottage** combines fun finishes with cushions covered in Cottage Dots fabric in ochre and shrimp.

These baskets from **Maine Cottage** are pretty and practical places to stash candles, napkins, and summer reading.

A wide range of colors gives this wicker furniture from **Maine Cottage** a playful look.

Attractive and affordable eucalyptus furniture from **Plow & Hearth** is a smart way to furnish your outdoor entertaining area.

The playful Harmony chaise from *Brown Jordan* can be arranged in a full-circle, as shown, or as a pair of half-circles.

Designer Richard Frinier translated the look of trans-oceanic yachts into a luxurious sectional offered by *Century Leisure,* covered—appropriate—in sailcloth.

The Stella cocktail table from *Maine Cottage* has old-fashioned charm, and the tomato color will brighten your patio or deck.

Crafted from durable Brazilian Cherry, this conversation set from *IGarden* is available with a 42" (107 cm) table, shown, or three other sizes.

Enjoy patio living in an all-weather wicker lounge like the Caribe reclining chaise from *Lloyd Flanders.*

This traditional wicker grouping from **Plow & Hearth** is made from UV-resistant extruded resin that's woven onto a sturdy aluminum frame for a worry-free, weatherproof performance.

Willowemoc furniture from **Orvis** has the look of classic wicker, but it's woven from polyresin-wrapped wire that will stand up to years of use (and abuse).

The Elegance collection of cast-aluminum furnishings from **Agio**.

For a rustic look, choose a rough-hewn piece like this twig table from **Orvis,** which has an antiqued pine top with a durable waxed finish.

For the fun of a swing, consider a glider, like this all-weather eucalyptus wood glider from **Plow & Hearth**.

SETTING THE PERFECT TABLE

Even an informal meal becomes something special when you set the table with coordinated linens from **Laura Ashley**.

These lobster napkins and placemats from **Orvis** are made from sturdy, washable cotton—a plus after a messy seafood dinner.

A personalized branding iron from **Orvis** allows you to sear letters onto your steak—choose your initials, or R, M, and W for Rare, Medium, and Well.

This glass lazy Susan from **Plow & Hearth** fits on any table—just slide your umbrella through its center hole.

Complete the lobster theme with **Orvis** lobster tumblers. Made from tough polycarbonate.

Dress up your table with a runner in a snappy pattern. This simple stripe from the **Zimmer + Rohde's** Summerhouse Collection is just the thing.

THE FINISHING TOUCH

The Diamante Portable Bar from *O.W. Lee* has a hideaway cutting board, tracks for hanging stemware, shelves, and a removable top.

Handmade in Turkey, this copper fireplace from *Orvis* has a food-safe grill so you can cook over wood or charcoal.

This outdoor fireplace from *Orvis* has an open design that can be viewed from all sides, plus a chimney that reduces smoke.

On chilly evenings, a portable heater like the BackHome Select stainless steel patio heater from *Coleman* will keep you cozy.

This beautiful copper fountain from **Plow & Hearth** has a classic silhouette and a state-of-the-art floating solar pump that will work in the sun without wiring.

The BackHome cooler from **Coleman** is attractive and designed to resist rust.

With compartments for fire-making essentials, the Wood Sling Rack from **L.L. Bean** keeps everything for your outdoor fireplace close at hand.

Position planters like these European-made wooden ones, in Natural (shown) or White, from **Plow & Hearth**, along the edge of your deck or patio for an elegant garden effect.

A few soft blankets and fabrics with a touchable quality, like these from **Laura Ashley**, will create a patio atmosphere of comfort and warmth.

An outdoor fan keeps air circulating in covered outdoor areas. The 28535 IE from **Hunter** in Dark Palm has a tropical air.

Personalize your outdoor living area with artwork, like this all-weather Avenue in the Garden print from **Plow & Hearth**.

These water-repellant cushions from **Plow & Hearth** have removable, washable covers that won't fade, mildew, or wash out.

Delight your guests with a whimsical copper wind sculpture from **Orvis**. Designed by artist Neil Sater.

CHAPTER SEVEN

YOU CAN DO IT

HANDS-ON PROJECTS THAT WILL
ENHANCE YOUR OUTDOOR COOKING SPACE

BY ANDREW KARRE

- MAKE A FREESTANDING ARBOR
- TILE A COUNTERTOP
- BUILD AN INDISPENSIBLE OUTDOOR KITCHEN CART

By now you've probably realized that the outdoor kitchens pictured in this book have a few things in common: they look great; they're stocked with all the latest appliances and materials; and (most of them) cost a lot of money. Lucky for you, it is possible to create a space of your own that shares the first two attributes, but not the third—if, that is, you're willing to take on some of the work yourself. If you head to your local home-improvement store, you'll likely find a rack of step-by-step instructions on building such outdoor kitchen necessities as a grill island. Or, try one (or all) of the projects we've included here—with a little careful planning and a few weekends' effort, they'll put you well on the way to the outdoor kitchen of your dreams.

MAKE A FREESTANDING ARBOR

Nothing can take the place of an arbor for lending a relaxed ambiance to a patio. This elegant design is not only simple to construct, but is also sturdy and freestanding. You can set it over a grill island or outdoor kitchen prep area, and hang a task light and utensils from it. You can use it in a seating area to cast welcome shade over a chair or chaise. Place it at the entrance to your patio and put a potted vine on either side to twine over it to create a charming entrance to your outdoor kitchen. The choice is yours, because the best part about this arbor is its portability.

MATERIALS

- wood glue
- wood sealer or stain
- #10 x 2½" (6 cm) wood screws
- ⅜"-dia. x 2½" (1 x 6 cm) lag screws (8)
- 6" (15 cm) lag screws (4)
- 2½" (6 cm) and 3" (8 cm) deck screws
- finishing materials

LUMBER

- 1" x 2" x 8' (3 x 5 x 20 cm) cedar (2)
- 2" x 2" x 8' (5 x 5 x 20 cm) cedar (5)
- 2" x 4" x 8' (5 x 10 x 20 cm) cedar (9)
- 2" x 6" x 8' (5 x 15 x 20 cm) cedar (3)

CUTTING LIST

A. leg front (4)	1½" x 3½" x 72" (4 x 9 x 183 cm) cedar
B. leg side (4)	1½" x 3½" x 72" (4 x 9 x 183 cm) cedar
C. cross beam (2)	1½" x 3½" x 36" (4 x 9 x 91 cm) cedar
D. top beam (2)	1½" x 5½" x 72" (4 x 14 x 183 cm) cedar
E. side rail (2)	1½" x 3½" x 21" (4 x 9 x 53 cm) cedar
F. side spreader (2)	1½" x 5½" x 21" (4 x 14 x 53 cm) cedar
G. trellis strip (9)	1½" x 1½" x 48" (4 x 4 x 122 cm) cedar
H. cross strip (15)	⅞" x 1½" x *" (2 x 4 x *cm) cedar
I. brace (4)	1½" x 5½" x 15" (4 x 14 x 38 cm) cedar

* = cut to fit

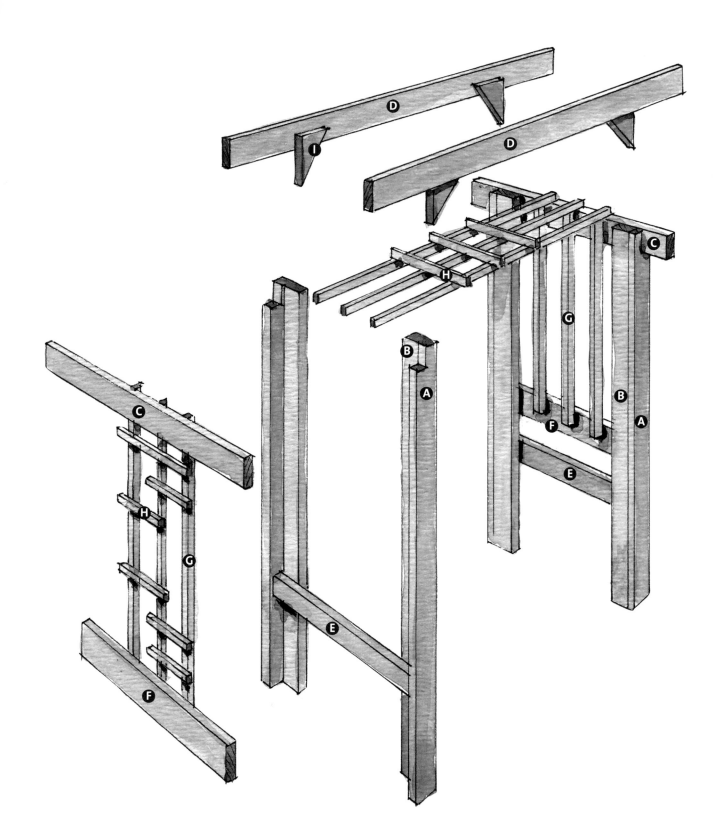

◀ STEP ONE

Make the legs. Each of legs is built from two 6' (2 m)-long cedar 2 x 4s (5 x 10 cm). Cut the leg fronts (A) and leg sides (B) to length. Attach the leg fronts and leg sides at right angles with wood glue and 3" (7.5 cm) deck screws (spaced every 12" [30.5 cm]); the tops and bottoms should be flush.

Use a jigsaw to cut a 3½" (9 cm)-long x 2" (5 cm)-wide notch at the top outside corner of each leg front (see illustration). These notches support the cross beams.

STEP TWO ▶

Make the cross beams, rails, and spreaders. Cut the cross beams (C) to length. Cut the spreaders (F) to length. The spreaders fit above the rails on each side. Cut the rails (E) to length. They fit between the leg pairs near the bottoms.

Assemble the two side frames. Each frame is made of two leg assemblies, a spreader, a cross beam, and a rail. Lay two leg assemblies parallel on a flat surface; space the assemblies so the inside faces of the notched leg boards are 21" (53.5 cm) apart (the length of the rail). Set a cross beam into the notches so there is 6" (15 cm) overhanging the legs on either side. Then, set a spreader and rail into the frame to keep the spacing.

Drill ⅜" (1 cm) pilot holes through the cross beam into the leg sides (two holes for each leg; see illustration). Counterbore all the holes, and drive in 2½" x ⅜" (6.5 x 1 cm) lag screws.

Position the spreader between the legs so its top is 25 ½" (65 cm) from the bottoms of the legs. Position the rail 18" (45.5 cm) above the leg bottoms. Drill and counterbore pilot holes through the spreader and rail and into the leg sides, taking care to keep the rail and stretcher square with the legs. Secure the pieces with glue and 3" (7.5 cm) deck screws.

Assemble the second side frame as above.

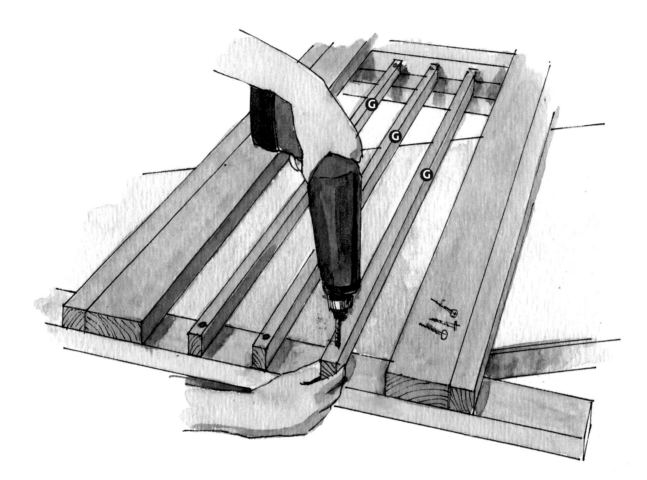

▲ STEP THREE

Attach the side trellis pieces. These components are the vertical pieces made from 2" x 2" (5 x 5 cm) pieces of cedar. Cut six trellis strips (G) to length. Space three on each side so they are 2⅜" (6 cm) apart, with ends flush with the top of the cross beam. Drill and counterbore pilot holes through each strip into the cross beam and spreader. Attach the strips with 2½" (6.5 cm) deck screws (see illustration).

Repeat on the second side frame.

STEP FOUR ▶

Cut the two top beams (D) to length.

Assemble the top and sides. Because the side assemblies are heavy, you'll want to brace them for easy assembly. Use a pair of 8' (2.5 m)-long 1 x 4s (2.5 x 10 cm) and clamps to connect the frames (see illustration). Clamp the braces so the tops and bottoms of the side frames are 52" (132 cm) apart. Use a level and plumb bob to ensure all corners are square.

Mark a center point for a lag bolt 10 ¾" (27.5 cm) from the end of each top beam. Through the top edge of each beam, drill ¼" (5 mm) pilot holes in the center of the edge so that the holes intersect the center point you just drew. Counterbore the holes for lag screws.

Position the top beam across the cross beams on one side so that the back face of the top beam is flush with the front face of the leg front, and so that overhang is equal on both sides. Transfer the pilot hole locations from the top beam to the cross beams. Remove the top beam, and drill ¼" (5 mm) pilot holes in the locations you just marked. Secure the top beam to the cross beams with 6" x ⅜" (15 x 1 cm) lag screws.

Repeat on the other side of the arbor assembly.

Cut the four braces (I). Cut two 15" (38 cm) pieces of 2 x 6 (5 x 15 cm) cedar. Cut the two pieces diagonally to form four triangles; these are the braces. Attach the braces to the joints where the leg fronts meet the top beams with 2 ½" (6.5 cm) deck screws. Verify that the whole assembly remains square.

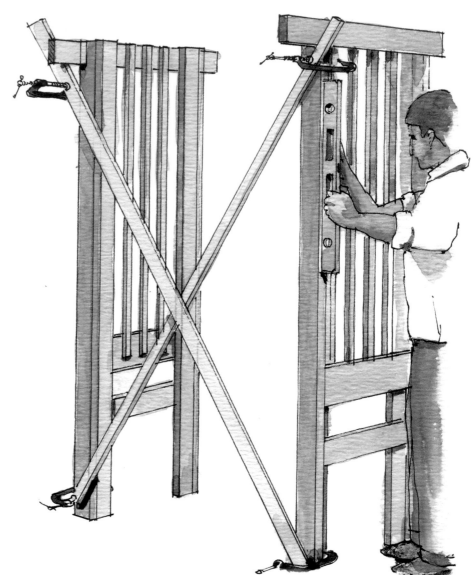

Cut three more trellis strips (G) to length. Space the strips between the top beams, 2 ⅜" (6 cm) apart, and attach them with 2 ½" (6.5 cm) deck screws.

Cut cross strips (H) to length as desired (you may want some to span all the trellis strips, and others to span only two). Space them as desired, and secure them to the sides and top with wood screws.

STEP FIVE

Apply a finish to the arbor. Protect the cedar with clear wood sealer.

After the finish has dried, move the arbor into place. It is stable enough to be freestanding on a hard, level surface like a stone or brick patio. On a deck, you may want to secure it to the deck boards with screws. Use metal stakes to secure it on soft ground.

TILE A COUNTERTOP

After the right grill, a capacious countertop is probably the most important element in an outdoor kitchen. You'll need plenty of room to prep foods, place hot pans, and plate up. If you'd like to do some of the work yourself, tiling the countertop around your grill is a fairly easy do-it-yourself project that you can probably complete in one to three weekends of work, depending on the size of the counter. Plan to work during dry weather when temperatures are between 40° and 85°F (5°–30°C). Here's how:

MATERIALS

- exterior-grade tiles (they must be freeze-thaw resistant; glazed tiles do not need sealing, but unglazed tiles do)
- wet saw with a diamond blade, tile cutter, or tile nipper
- safety glasses
- mastic adhesive
- thin-set mortar
- three-part sanded epoxy grout
- grout float
- bucket of clean rinse water
- heavy-duty scouring pad
- sponge
- plastic spacers
- plastic sheeting
- penetrating water-based grout sealant

STEP ONE

Whether you're tiling a newly built countertop or updating an existing one, you'll need to prepare the surface. Existing laminate or concrete countertops must be cleaned and roughed up before you can cover them with tile. Do not apply tile directly to a wooden countertop. The best substrate for a tile countertop is a double layer of outdoor plywood screwed together and topped with cement board nailed to the plywood with roofing nails.

▼ STEP TWO

Beginning with the backsplash, lay out or dry-fit the tiles in a diamond or horizontal pattern. Start to attach the tiles at a reference line in the center of your project, so that any cut tiles will be balanced on each end of the backsplash. Snap a chalk line to mark your reference point, and get started. Wearing safety glasses, use a wet saw (available at equipment-rental stores), tile cutter, or tile nipper to cut tiles to fit, if necessary.

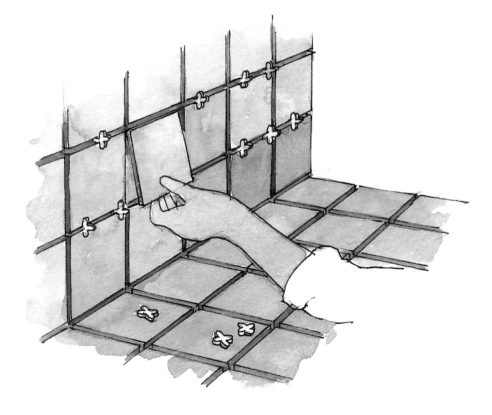

◄ STEP THREE

Apply mastic adhesive to the back-splash with a notched trowel (your tile store will supply you with the appropriate trowel and mastic), spreading only as much as you can cover with tiles in a few minutes. Place the tiles, taking care to keep the grout lines even and straight. As you place each tile, tap it gently to embed it in the adhesive.

STEP FOUR ►

For even grout lines, insert plastic cross-shape spacers between tiles as you set them.

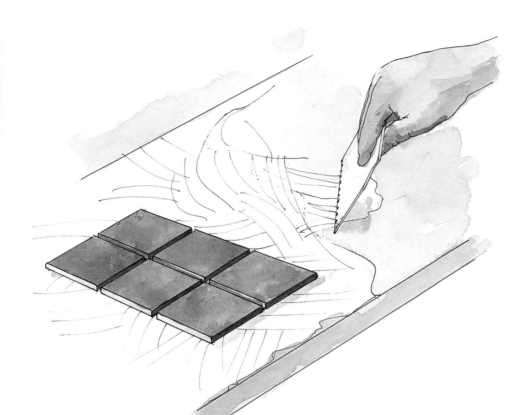

◀ **STEP FIVE**
For the countertop, follow the same basic procedure, but use thin-set mortar instead of mastic—it's more durable and water-resistant.

STEP SIX ▶
When the counter tiles are set, place bull-nose tiles along the front of the countertop, or for a square-edged look, cut tiles to fit. Spread thin-set mortar on the back of the edging tiles, and set them in place along the counter's edge.

STEP SEVEN

Allow the mastic and thin-set mortar to dry overnight, and then mix the grout according to the manufacturer's directions. Use a weather-resistant, three-part sanded epoxy grout, and work in 4' (122 cm) sections, because grout hardens quickly.

◀ STEP EIGHT

With a grout float, spread the grout onto the tiles using a diagonal, sweeping motion, and push it into the grout lines. Wipe frequently with a heavy-duty scouring pad to remove excess grout from the surface of the tiles, rinsing the pad as you work.

STEP NINE ▶

Follow up by wiping the counters with a clean, damp sponge. Cover the counter with plastic sheeting for a few days while the grout cures, and then apply a penetrating water-based sealer. This sealer will protect the grout from staining and damage.

◀ STEP TEN

When the sealer dries, buff the tiles to a shine with a clean, lint-free cloth

BUILD AN INDISPENSABLE OUTDOOR KITCHEN CART

There never seems to be enough counterspace in a busy kitchen, whether indoors or out, but you can solve that problem with this weather-wise kitchen cart on wheels. You'll have plenty of counterspace on hand, whether you need it grillside or tableside, or as a portable bar. By fastening a towel rack at either end, you can wheel around the cart by the "handle" or use it as a place to park your towel and barbecue tongs. This project can be made easily in half a day with pieces of standard lumber and hardware.

MATERIALS

- circular saw
- drill
- clamps
- carpenter's square
- socket wrenches
- cedar lumber
- stainless-steel deck screws
- eight 3½" x ³⁄₁₆" (9 x 0.5 cm) stainless-steel lag bolts with nuts and washers
- four locking casters
- nontoxic sanding sealer or paint (if desired)
- ceramic tile materials (see Tile a Countertop, page 148)

CUTTING LIST

A.	legs (4)	2" x 6" (5 x 15 cm) cedar	30" (76 cm)
B.	top crossbraces (2)	2" x 6" (5 x 15 cm) cedar	31" (79 cm)
C.	bottom crossbraces (2)	2" x 6" (5 x 15 cm) cedar	32 ½" (82.5 cm)
D.	crossbrace blocking (4)	2" x 6" (5 x 15 cm) cedar	12" (30.5 cm)
E.	caster-mount blocking (4)	2" x 6" (5 x 15 cm) cedar	5½" (14 cm)
F.	counter substrate (1)	¾" (2 cm) exterior plywood	48" x 33" (122 x 84 cm)
G.	counter support (2)*	2" x 6" (5 x 15 cm) cedar	48" (122 cm)
H.	lower shelf planks (4)	2" x 6" (5 x 15 cm) cedar	22" (56 cm)
I.	front apron support (1)*	2" x 4" (5 x 10 cm) cedar	52" (132 cm)
J.	front apron (1)	1" x 8" (2.5 x 20.5 cm) cedar	66" (167.5 cm)
K.	towel rod blocks (2)	1" x 6" (2.5 x 15 cm) cedar	6" x 3" (15 x 7.5 cm)
L.	towel rod (1)	¾" (2 cm) dowel	32" (81.5 cm)

* shown on page 154

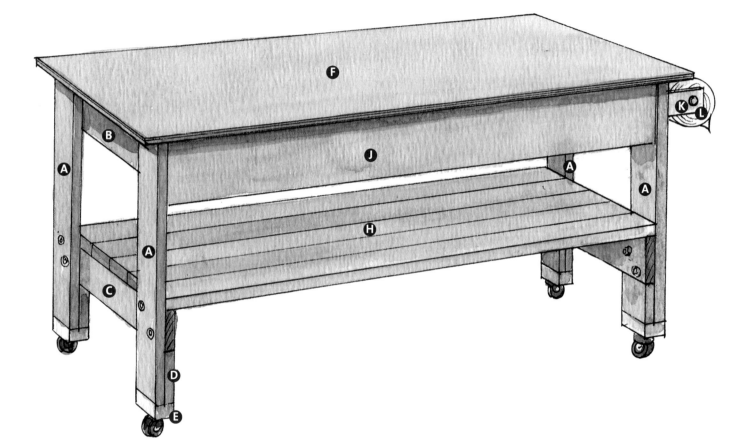

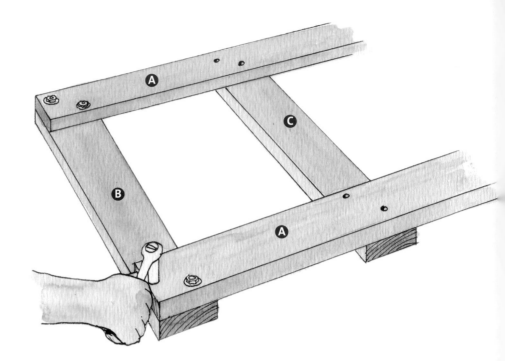

▶ STEP ONE

Cut the legs (A), crossbrace blocking (D), crossbraces (B, C), and caster-mount blocking (E) to size. Set a crossbrace block on each leg, face to face, with edges and bottoms flush. Drill pilot holes, and secure the crossbrace blocking to the legs by drilling four deck screws into each leg.

Then, set the legs on a work surface, spaced 33" (84 cm) apart. Lay out the top and bottom crossbraces on the legs. Position the bottom crossbrace so that its edge is tight to the tops of the crossbrace blocking and its ends are flush with the outer edges of the legs. Next, set the top crossbrace so that its top edge is flush with the top ends of the legs, and it is centered on the legs (leave 1½" (4 cm) of setback from the outer edge of each leg on both sides). Check the assembly for square, and clamp it in place.

Drill two ¼" (5 mm) pilot holes at each joint. Then, thread 3½" x ³⁄₁₆" (9 x 0.5 cm) lag bolts through the holes. Slide on a washer for each, and tighten the nuts. Check again for square, and then remove the clamps. Set a caster block on the bottom of each leg, and secure it with four deck screws. Repeat steps 1 through 3 for the other side of the assembly.

◀ STEP TWO

Cut the counter substrate plywood (F) to size. Along the short sides, mark lines 4½" (11.5 cm) inset from the edges. Position the counter supports (G) inside the lines. The supports should be flush with the substrate's back edge but 2" (5 cm) inset from the front. Secure the supports to the substrate with deck screws. Set the front apron support (I) between the counter supports, so that its outer edge is flush with the front ends of the counter supports. Secure the apron support with deck screws.

▼ STEP THREE

Set the counter substrate (F) upside down on a work surface. Place a side on each end so that the top cross-brace (B) is snug against the counter support (G) and the back edges of the legs (A) are flush with the back edge of the counter supports. Clamp the crossbrace in place, and use the carpenter's square to be sure that the legs are square.

On each side, drive eight evenly spaced deck screws through the top crossbrace into the counter support.

Set the front apron (J) between the legs and against the front apron support. Secure it by driving two deck screws through each leg into the edge of the apron. Then, drive 12 evenly spaced screws through the face of the apron into the front apron support.

While the cart is upside down, install locking casters on the caster blocking on each leg. Follow the caster manufacturer's instructions.

Flip the cart upright. Cut the apron to size. Set the apron between the legs and tight against the apron support. Clamp it in place, and then secure it with three deck screws driven through each leg and six evenly spaced deck screws driven down through the substrate.

STEP FOUR

Cut the lower shelf planks to length, and rip one of the planks down to 5" (12.5 cm) wide.

Set the cart on its legs and lock the casters. Set each plank across the bottom crossbraces. The planks should sit flush with the outer edges of the bottom crossbraces, and they should be centered between the legs. Check that the cart is square, and then secure the planks with two deck screws through each plank end.

Cut the towel blocks to size. Mark a point 2" (5 cm) in from a short edge and centered between the long edges on each block. Drill a ¾" (2 cm) hole through each block at the marking.

Choose a side of the cart for the towel rod. Set both towel rod blocks under the counter substrate so that the short edge opposite the hole is tight to the crossbrace and the outer face of the block is flush with the inner edge of a leg. Clamp the blocks in place, and secure them with two wood screws driven into the legs and one through the substrate into the top of each block. Thread the dowel thought the holes. (If you want a towel rod on both ends of the cart, repeat the steps above on the other end of the cart.)

STEP FIVE

Seal or paint the lower part of the assembly, if desired. Finish the work surface of this cart with ceramic tile. Follow the instruction on page 148 for installing tile, omitting the backsplash.

RESOURCES

DESIGN PROFESSIONALS

Chris Barrett
Chris Barrett Design, Inc.
1640 19th Street
Santa Monica, CA USA 90404
310.586.0773
www.chrisbarrettdesign.com

Michael Glassman
Michael Glassman & Associates
Landscape Design & Consulting
916.736.2222
www.michaelglassman.com

Larry Malesky
Fireplace & BBQ Center
Lyons Business Park
6601 Lyons Road
Coconut Creek, FL USA 33070
954.428.2606
www.fireplace-bbq.com

Mary Jo Peterson
Mary Jo Peterson, Inc.
3 Sunset Cove Road
Brookfield, CT USA 06804
203.775.4765
www.mjpdesign.com

Steve Straughan
Kirkpatrick Associates Architects, Inc.
4201 Redwood Avenue
Los Angeles, CA USA 90066
310.821.1400
www.kaa-arch.com

MANUFACTURERS

Agio International
800.416.3511
www.agio-usa.com
Outdoor furniture

American Marazzi Tile
Headquarters & Manufacturing Plant
359 Clay Road
Sunnyvale, TX USA 75182
972.226.0110
www.marazzitile.com
Multicolored patterned tiles

Aussie Grill Company
1500 Industrial Road
Greeneville, TN USA 37745
800.251.7558
www.aussiegrill.com
Gourmet grills

Barbecues Galore
800.752.3085
www.bbqgalore.com
Grills, smokers, accessories

BBQ Factory
90 Dorley Street
Mona Vale NSW
Australia 2103
02.9999.1891
www.bbqfactory.com.au
Barbeques grills, furniture, accessories

Big Green Egg
3417 Lawrenceville Highway
Tucker, GA USA 30084
770.938.9394
www.biggreenegg.com
Ceramic smokers

The Brinkmann Corp.
4215 McEwen Road
Dallas, TX USA 75244
800.468.5252 ext. 430
www.thebrinkmanncorp.com
Grills, smokers, and more

Brown Jordan
www.brownjordan.com
Outdoor furniture

Century Furniture
800.852.5552
www.centuryfurniture.com
Outdoor furniture

Ceramiche Fontana Bismantova
www.rondinegroup.com
www.italiantiles.com
Italian ceramic tiles

Cinders Barbecues Ltd.
High Bentham
Lancaster LA2 7NB
United Kingdom
0.152.425.2900
cindersbarbecues.co.uk
Grills and accessories

Coleman
3600 North Hydraulic
Wichita, KS USA 67219
800.835.3278
www.coleman.com
Grills, stoves, outdoor accessories

Concrete Network
www.concretenetwork.com
*Concrete patios with optional
decorative accents*

Crossville, Inc.
P.O. Box 1168
Crossville, TN USA 38557
931.484.2110
www.crossvilleinc.com
All-weather tile

Edimax-Gruppo Beta SpA
www.edimax.it
www.italiantiles.com
All-weather tile

Frontgate
5566 West Chester Road
West Chester, OH USA 45069
888.263.9850
www.frontgate.com
Grills, patio furniture, accessories

GE
800.626.2005
www.geappliances.com
Outdoor appliances

Gloster Furniture
UK: 44 (0) 117 931 5335
USA: 888-GLOSTER
www.gloster.com
Teak outdoor furniture

Hammacher Schlemmer
800.321.1484
www.hammacher.com
Insect repellant devices

Heat & Glo
A Brand of Hearth & Home
Technologies Inc.
Corporate Office
20802 Kensington Boulevard
Lakeville, MN USA 55044
888.427.3973
www.heat-n-glo.com
Grills, fireplaces, accessories

Hunter Fan
888.830.1326
www.hunterfan.com
Weather-proof ceiling fans

IGarden
800-688-2882
www.igardencasual.com
Outdoor furniture and accessories

Jenn-Air
Maytag Corporation
403 W. 4th Street North
Newton, IA USA 50208
800.688.1100
www.jennair.com
Outdoor appliances

Kamado Corporation
East Coast: 877.627.2549
Pacific: 877.257.6871
www.kamado.com
Ceramic barbeque grills

Kettler International, Inc.
P. O. Box 2747
Virginia Beach, VA USA 23450
757.427.2400
www.kettlerusa.com
Outdoor furniture

**KitchenAid Customer
Satisfaction Center**
P.O. Box 218
St. Joseph, MI USA 49085
800.422.1230
www.kitchenaid.com
Outdoor appliances

Lloyd/Flanders
www.lloydflanders.com
Outdoor furniture

Laneventure
P.O. Box 849
Conover, NC USA 28613
800.235.3558
www.laneventure.com
Outdoor furniture

Lasertron
14251 Northwest 4 Street
Sunrise, FL USA 33325
954.846.8600
www.lasertrondirect.com
Stainless steel kitchen products

Laura Ashley
27 Bagleys Lane
Fulham SW6 2QA
United Kingdom
0871.9835.999
www.lauraashley.com
Fabric, lighting, furnishings, accessories

Lennox
Richardson, TX USA 75080
800-9-LENNOX
www.lennox.com
Hearth products and air conditioning

Magma Grills
Calor Corp.
Tachenbrook Park
Athena Drive
Warwick CV34 6RL
United Kingdom
0.800.917.1272
www.barbecue-online.co.uk
Grills and accessories

Maine Cottage
888.859.5522
www.mainecottage.com
Colorful home furnishings, textiles

Marazzi Tile
www.marazzitile.com
Coordinating floor and wall tile

Marvel
P.O. Box 997
Richmond, IN USA 47375
800.428.6644
www.lifeluxurymarvel.com
Outdoor refrigerator, beverage coolers

Masterbuilt Outdoor Products
450 Brown Avenue
Columbus, GA USA 31906
800.489.1581 ext. 101
www.masterbuilt.com
Cookers, fryers, accessories

Modern Home Products
150 South Ram Road
Antioch, IL USA 60002
888.647.4745
www.modernhomeproducts.com
Gas grills, and accessories

Napoleon Gourmet Grills
www.napoleongrills.com
*Gourmet grills, barbeque accessories and
outdoor living products*

Orvis
888.235.9763
www.orvis.com
*Home accents including furniture,
floor covering, lighting, and candles*

O. W. Lee
1822 East Francis Street
Ontario, CA USA 91761
800.776.9533
www.owlee.com
Outdoor furniture

Patio Companion
The Companion Group
401 Roland Way, Suite 250
Oakland, CA 94621 USA
800.521.0505
www.companion-group.com
Accessories, bug control products

Pest-Control.bz
www.pest-control.bz
High-frequency animal repellant

Plow & Hearth
800.494.7544
www.plowhearth.com
*Home furnishings, lighting,
outdoor living accessories*

REI
www.rei.com
Bear canisters

Sunbrella
336.227.6211
www.sunbrella.com
Outdoor fabrics

Terra Furniture
626.912.8523
www.terrafurniture.com
Outdoor furniture

Thermador
5551 McFadden Avenue
Huntington Beach, CA USA 92649
800.656.9226
www.thermador.com
Outdoor appliances

Vermont Castings
CFM Specialty Home Products
410 Admiral Boulevard
Mississauga, Ontario L5T 2N6
Canada
905.670.7777
www.vermontcastings.com
Grills, accessories

Vintage Grills
39740 Garand Lane
Palm Desert, CA USA 92211
800.998.8966
www.vintage-grills.com
Grills, accessories

Viking Range
111 Front Street
Greenwood, MS USA 38930
888.VIKING1
www.vikingrange.com
Outdoor appliances

Weber-Stephen Co.
200 East Daniels Road
Palatine, IL USA 60067-6266
800.446.1071
www.weber.com/bbq
Gills, accessories

Zimmer + Rohde
Zimmersmühlenweg 14-18
61440 Oberursel/Frankfurt
Deutschland
0.6171.632.02
www.zimmer-rohde.com
*Ardecora, Etamine, Summerhouse, Möbel
textile collections*

PROFESSIONAL HELP

**American Society of Landscape
Architects (ASLA)**
*For a unique perspective on how the interior
and exterior of your home work together,
consult a landscape architect. To find one,
visit www.asla.org*

ISH Worldwide
Frankfurt, North America, China, the Middle East
http://ish.messefrankfurt.com/global/en/home.html
*ISH Messe Frankfurt is the world's largest
and foremost exhibition for the kitchen and
bathroom trade sectors. ISH Frankfurt has
over the years overseen the creation of a
number of highly successful daughter events
around the world such as ISH China and ISH
North America*

**The National Association
of Home Builders (NAHB)**
*To find a builder with experience in outdoor
kitchen design and construction, visit
www.nahb.org, the website
of the NAHB*

The National Association of the Remodeling Industry (NARI)
*If you're looking for a professional remodeler, NARI's website, www.nari.org, is a great
place to start*

National Kitchen & Bathroom Assn. (NZ) Inc.
Papamoa, Bay of Plenty, New Zealand
*Certified kitchen designers with the know-how
to achieve practical, well-planned kitchen
designs. Contact them by phone
(09004.NKBA) or visit their website,
http://www.nkba.org.nz*

**The National Kitchen & Bath Assn.
(NKBA)**
*This not-for-profit trade organization's website offers a wealth of kitchen and bath
design information and allows consumers to
search their member listing for local professionals. Visit www.nkba.org*

PHOTOGRAPHER CREDITS

ABOUT THE AUTHOR

Amanda Lecky is the editor of *House Beautiful Kitchens/ Baths Magazine* and the former editor of *House Beautiful Home Remodeling & Decorating Magazine.* She is a frequent contributor to magazines such as *Country Living, Good Housekeeping, This Old House,* and *Renovation Style.* She lives in New York with her husband and two sons, and does all her outdoor cooking in the Adirondacks. This is her first book.

ACKNOWLEDGMENTS

My thanks to all the talented professionals whose advice and expertise helped as I wrote this book. The chefs I interviewed—Rick Browne, Paula Deen, George Hirsch, Steve Raichlen, Dwayne Ridgaway, Richard Sandoval, and John Stage—were so generous with their time and ideas, often stealing a few minutes for the interview from their busy taping (and cooking) schedules. And the design professionals were no less enthusiastic about sharing their experience, so thank you again to Chris Barrett, Michael Glassman, Larry Malesky, Mary Jo Peterson, and Steve Straughan. To Delilah Smittle, my editor, and Betsy Gammons, the photo editor who gathered so many beautiful images for the book and shepherded the project through its various twists and turns, my gratitude for making my first book such a fun, collaborative experience. Of course, this book wouldn't be nearly so interesting without all those gorgeous photographs, so a heartfelt thanks to the many photographers who supplied their images and manufacturers who allowed us to feature their products. And finally, thanks to my husband, who tended the grill while I wrote about it.